Copyright Wilhelm 2024

Email: wilhelm@wilhelmbooks.co.za
https://wilhelmbooks.co.za

Cover Design and Illustrator: Linta Anish ~ linsaraillustration

Sakura Book Publishing, Durban, South Africa
www.sakurabookpublishing.com
alta@sakurabookpublishing.com

ISBN: 978-1-0370-1840-4(print)
978-1-0370-1841-1(e-book)

All rights reserved. No part of this publication may be reproduced, distributed, or transmitted in any form or any means, including photocopying, recordings, or other electronic or mechanical methods without the prior written permission of the author, except in the case of brief quotations embodied in critical reviews and certain noncommercial uses permitted by copyright law.

# The Cult's Tentacles
## Wilhelm

# Wilhelm

Born in Windhoek, where the vast desert winds whisper stories of resilience, the author's early years were steeped in the open skies and rugged landscapes of Namibia.

But it was the old Western Transvaal, where he grew up and studied, that truly shaped the man he would become. There, beneath the endless sun, life was a mix of tradition and quiet determination—qualities that would later echo in his writing.

**The Cult's Tentacles**

The octopus, with its eight snaking arms, is a formidable predator. Once it sets its sights on you, escape is nearly impossible. Similarly, a cult can be just as suffocating, making it difficult for its victims to break free. Forty years ago, I embarked on a journey with my wife, both of us eager to serve the Lord. Like many other couples before us, we were searching for a church where we could devote ourselves to God. Little did we know, that innocent quest would lead us, unwittingly, into the belly of a beast far more dangerous than we could have imagined. It started simply enough with an invitation to a play at a local church. The members

**The Cult's Tentacles**

greeted us with overwhelming warmth, and we immediately felt at ease. By the end of the evening, they had invited us to attend the following Sunday service, and we accepted, swept up by their friendliness.

When we arrived that Sunday, we were struck by an odd sight. All the men stood in a row, forming a circle around the entrance. They were dressed in dark suits, exuding an unsettling uniformity. A young man, about our age, stepped forward and introduced himself. He seemed pleasant enough and led us inside, introducing us to various members of the congregation

**The Cult's Tentacles**

as we went along. We met underdeacons, priests, and brothers, all of whom held some apparent position of importance. My wife was introduced to the women inside the foyer, all addressed as "Sister So-and-So." She joined them, while I remained with the men outside. The use of "Brother" or "Sister" without using first names can sometimes be seen as a way to diminish individuality and assert control. I began to notice that whenever a new couple arrived, the entire group would turn to greet them in perfect unison. It was as though they were part of some choreographed routine. One couple, in particular,

**The Cult's Tentacles**

caught my eye. The man was introduced to me as "Elder." His importance was palpable, as everyone, even those lingering outside, rushed to greet him and his wife. There was a clear hierarchy at play, and even in that moment, I could feel the weight of the Elder's influence settling over us. Once everyone had been introduced, we were led to our seats. As we took our places in the pews, the entire congregation stood. The Elder made his way to the pulpit followed by a group of men who trailed behind him in a solemn procession. It was as if he were leading a parade of devout followers, and the moment felt heavy

**The Cult's Tentacles**

with unspoken reverence. The congregation sat, except for the first few rows, which were occupied by the choir. Their voices swelled in perfect harmony, sending shivers down my spine. I glanced at my wife and saw her enraptured by the singing. We had no idea that this would be our first step into a world that would ensnare us for years to come. As I sat there, absorbing the unfamiliar surroundings, one thing stood out: the Elder's constant references to someone called "the Apostle." Almost every sentence he spoke began with "the Apostle says" or "the Apostle wants." It quickly became clear that the Apostle was the true

**The Cult's Tentacles**

power behind the scenes, the one pulling all the strings. After the service, the congregation gathered for coffee and eats. The Elder approached me again, showing a strange interest in my life. He bombarded me with questions. Where did I work? Where did we live? Was our home ours or did we rent? At the time, I brushed it off as friendly curiosity, but looking back, I now realize that he was calculating my potential tithe payments. The tithe system, I would soon learn, was one of the most insidious arms of the Octopus. Disguised as a way to show your trustworthy," it was really a method for the church to exert

**The Cult's Tentacles**

financial control over its members. But at that time, I was still naive, still basking in the warm glow of their camaraderie. As we mingled, shaking hands and exchanging pleasantries, I couldn't help but feel a sense of belonging. My wife and I were welcomed so warmly, and the Elder's questions seemed so harmless. Little did I know, the Octopus had already begun wrapping its tendrils around us, pulling us deeper into its grasp. It would take years before I realized just how tightly it held on—and how difficult it would be to escape.

**The Cult's Tentacles**

It was a quiet Thursday evening, just days after our first visit to the church, when I heard an unexpected knock at the door. Upon opening it, I found two men standing on our porch, their suits starched to a crisp perfection that seemed almost unnatural. I recognized the younger of the two immediately—the same man who had introduced us to the congregation during that initial service. He greeted me with a smile that exuded warmth and familiarity. "Underdeacon," he said, introducing himself formally. His companion, a slightly older man, nodded politely as he was introduced as "Brother. "I invited them inside. My wife, ever the

**The Cult's Tentacles**

gracious hostess, exchanged pleasantries as we settled into the living room. The Underdeacon began with what seemed like a thoughtful gesture, explaining that they had come to see if we had any questions or concerns about the service we'd attended. At the time, I saw it as a sign of the church's care for its flock, a sincere effort to ensure our spiritual growth. But now, looking back through the lens of hindsight, I can see there was more to it than simple courtesy. They had come to solidify the church's hold over us, to make sure that we wouldn't slip away. The visit wasn't just a polite follow-up; it was an

**The Cult's Tentacles**

expertly orchestrated move to ensure we were firmly in the Octopus' grasp. Each word they spoke, each glance they exchanged, was a carefully calculated attempt to sow the seeds of loyalty and trust. As the conversation meandered, they asked about our impressions of the Sunday service, especially of the Elder's sermon. Their eyes gleamed with a peculiar intensity as they listened to our responses, as if probing for any sign of uncertainty or doubt. My wife and I caught in their spell of warmth and sincerity didn't recognize what was happening. We had been drawn into their world—oblivious to the manipulations

**The Cult's Tentacles**

unfolding right in front of us. At one point, the Underdeacon asked if we had a Bible that he could use to illustrate something. I felt a flicker of embarrassment as I admitted I'd never owned one. My wife hurried to fetch her old Bible, the only one in the house, a relic from before our marriage. The Underdeacon's eyes gleamed as he took the bible, his fingers gently caressing its worn cover. Flipping to Ephesians, Chapter 4, Verse 11, he began to read aloud: "And he gave some, apostles; and some, prophets; and some, evangelists; and some, pastors and teachers..." I had no way of knowing at that moment just

**The Cult's Tentacles**

how pivotal this passage would become. It would later be drilled into my mind as a cornerstone of the church's doctrine, one that I would, in time, use to persuade others in my stead. The Underdeacon went on to explain that their church alone possessed these gifts—apostles, prophets, and teachers. According to him, no other church in the world held this divine authority. All others were misguided, lacking the true spiritual leadership that only their community could provide. My wife and I exchanged startled glances. The claim was bold, audacious even, but it

**The Cult's Tentacles**

intrigued us. How could we ignore such confidence, such certainty?

After they left, my wife and I spent hours discussing the visit, our excitement palpable. We talked of the sense of belonging the church seemed to offer, a community that welcomed us with open arms. Surely there was something special here, something unique. With a sense of anticipation, we resolved to return the following Sunday, eager to learn more. In retrospect, I realize just how deeply we had already fallen into the cult's grasp. We were being played—our fears, our desires, our longing for purpose, all

**The Cult's Tentacles**

expertly manipulated. The leaders knew exactly how to appeal to us, to reel us in. But at the time, we were blind to the signs, innocent and unaware of the perilous path we had started down

Sunday morning arrived with an unusual sense of urgency in the air. My wife seemed different today, as if something had stirred excitement within her. She was already bathed, her hair neatly brushed, and it wasn't even eight yet. I climbed out of bed, stretching away the remnants of sleep, and like any other Sunday, made my way to the dining table. The table was

**The Cult's Tentacles**

set, my usual bowl of cornflakes waiting patiently beside a jug of milk, though the day already felt anything but usual. Normally, we ate together, taking our time before heading out to do some shopping. Sundays were always slow, deliberate, but today was not like any other Sunday. Little did I know, this would be the first of many I didn't particularly feel like going to church today? My feet dragged, my mood sluggish, weighed down by the stillness of the early morning. But before I could dwell on it much longer, my wife came rushing out of the bedroom, her voice filled with unusual energy. "Hurry up! I don't

**The Cult's Tentacles**

want to be late!" she chirped, her eyes darting to the clock and then back at me, the intensity in her gaze catching me off guard. "Why?" I muttered to myself, glancing at the clock. Surely, they wouldn't start the service without us. The thought seemed ridiculous, but I kept quiet, not wanting to stir the pot or trigger a discussion so early. After finishing my breakfast, I reluctantly headed for the shower. The hot water helped wake me up, but something still felt off, like a wrong note played in an otherwise familiar tune. As I dressed, I reached for my tie, fumbling with the knot, my frustration growing as the silk slipped through my fingers. That's

**The Cult's Tentacles**

when she appeared again, this time clutching her hat, a delicate thing with a wide brim. "Do you think my hat should sit more on the back of my head?" she asked, tilting it this way and that, searching for approval. Before I could answer, she shifted it again, this time cocked slightly to the side. "Or maybe it should sit like this. What do you think?" I opened my mouth to respond, but she moved it once more. "What about like this?" Her eyes locked onto mine, waiting expectantly for some form of validation. "That looks fine," I muttered, unsure if it was the right answer or if she even heard me. The

**The Cult's Tentacles**

words felt hollow, but there was no stopping her now. I didn't understand the sudden fuss over a hat. The peace and quiet of our usual Sunday routine had vanished, swept away by this new, unnecessary urgency. Meanwhile, I was still wrestling with my tie, the knot slipping loose in my hands. I could feel my patience slipping too. She must have sensed it, because she stepped forward, her usual soft smile returning as she gently took the tie from my hands. Her fingers moved gracefully, and before I knew it, the knot was perfect, resting neatly at my collar. She gave me a quick peck on the cheek before disappearing back to

**The Cult's Tentacles**

the mirror to finish her makeup. I stood there for a moment, staring out the window of our small bedroom, the weight of the morning pressing down on me. Was this how it would be from now on? Every Sunday filled with restless energy, this strange preoccupation with the smallest, most trivial details? I couldn't help but wonder. Little did I know, it was only the beginning? This restless routine, this fuss over nothing, would become our pattern, a Quiet rhythm that would last for forty long years.
Work and church became the rhythm of our days, a relentless cycle that left

**The Cult's Tentacles**

no space for anything else. Family gatherings, friendships, hobbies, even a simple walk in the evening sun—all of it slowly vanished from our lives. We were consumed; wholly devoted to the idea that salvation was something we had to earn, step by step, duty by duty. "You must work for salvation." That phrase echoed through every sermon, every whispered conversation in the pews. It wasn't enough to just believe—you had to be present, active, part of every church event. Attendance wasn't optional; it was a mandate. To miss a meeting, to skip a task, even for a moment of rest, was unthinkable. To be absent was to slip away from the

**The Cult's Tentacles**

path, to invite the judgment of not just God but the people around you. Looking back now, it's clear to me that this was one of the tentacles that held us fast, that wrapped around us like a beast, suffocating any free will. The officers—each with their own ranks, from the mighty apostle to the humble underdeacon—watched over us, always reminding us of our place. They called it love, guidance, but I see now it was control. Subtle at first, but complete. The most powerful of those tentacles, the one that coiled tightest around us, was the tithes. "No tithes, no salvation."That wasn't just a warning—it was the law. Give ten per

**The Cult's Tentacles**

cent of your gross income or you were damned. No compromise, no excuse. It wasn't just about money; it was about proving your loyalty, your faith. To hold back even a penny was to declare yourself unfaithful, to seal your fate in the fires of hell. Karen and I were blind to it then, too blind to see how deeply we were entangled in the beast's grip. We believed, with all our hearts, that every sacrifice we made, every dollar we gave, every moment we spent in service, was necessary. Salvation was on the line, or so we thought. But now, when I close my eyes and think of those days, it's like watching myself from a distance. I see two people

**The Cult's Tentacles**

drowning, caught in the grasp of something far larger than they ever understood. We didn't see the octopus then, how it wrapped its tentacles around our minds, how it fed on our fears and insecurities. We were brainwashed—there's no softer word for it. Every doubt, every flicker of unease, was smothered by the weight of that single word: salvation. Some days, the burden felt too heavy. We'd lie awake at night, feeling it press down on us, that creeping sense of exhaustion, of being stretched too thin. But even then, we couldn't let go. We couldn't let ourselves question it. We just tightened our grip and pressed on,

**The Cult's Tentacles**

believing that if we could just work hard enough, give enough, do enough—we'd make it.

Day to day, life drifted into a rhythm so steady, it felt almost mechanical. Each morning, I'd lace my shoes, tuck my collar, and slip into the hum of the everyday—the same faces, the same streets, the same measured exchanges. But with every passing month, we saw less of our extended family. It wasn't intentional, really. But every time they called, eager for a visit, we'd be off somewhere—caught up in another activity, another event, another meeting. Judy was already in high

**The Cult's Tentacles**

school now, growing up fast, though sometimes it felt like I was watching from a distance. We were deep into church life. Our fellow members had become more than just acquaintances—they were our friends, our second family. Over time, my responsibilities within the church grew. I was a priest now, entrusted with the spiritual care of 20 households. It was a heavy, yet sacred, weight on my shoulders. Time seemed to slip through my fingers like sand; one moment, I was just another congregant, and now I had people looking to me for guidance. The elder, my overseer, was the one I reported to, but more often than not, it

**The Cult's Tentacles**

felt like I was reporting to the weight of tradition itself. Outside of the church, work had its own set of responsibilities. After Tom was promoted to district auditor, I slid into his old role as branch supervisor. It felt like a natural progression, though not without its challenges. I had to keep reminding myself that we priests didn't receive a salary from the church. Only the apostles did—and theirs was a salary to envy. Company, cars, a generous housing allowance, and a 13th pay check just in time for the year-end holidays. It felt distant from my own humble standing. Sure, the overseer, evangelist, and prophet had

**The Cult's Tentacles**

their travel expenses reimbursed, and some of the elders received similar compensation. But for the rest of us, we served with little expectation of material reward. Every year before sealing services, the church's focus shifted. New members. That was the goal. More members meant more tithes, and that had become the undercurrent of our lives, whether we spoke of it openly or not. Forty years of service, and looking back, it was clear that growth—numerical, financial—had been the guiding force.

It was a Wednesday, and I was coming home from work a little later than

**The Cult's Tentacles**

usual. The table was already set, a sign that Karen had been preparing dinner, and as I walked in, Judy came out of her room to greet me. We hugged and kissed, while Karen rushed out from the kitchen, planting a kiss on my cheek. The warmth of home was always a comfort, but tonight, something felt different. "We're running late," Karen said quickly, "its breadbreak and you need to lead the evening." Breadbreak, our weekly gathering, had become a tradition, and it often left us scrambling for time. We sat down to eat, but the air felt tense. "My mom called," Karen began after a few bites. Her voice was quieter than

**The Cult's Tentacles**

usual, and I immediately knew something was wrong. "She said my dad is seriously ill, but he refuses to go to the hospital. Your mom thinks... she thinks he won't make it through the week. "I paused, the weight of her words sinking in. "Is it that serious?" I asked, though deep down I knew it was. Karen nodded. "I think we should go there right after breadbreak," I suggested "But my homework isn't finished," Judy piped up, a slight frown creasing her forehead. "We don't have any other time, sweetheart," I said gently. Judy sighed, but didn't argue further. Looking back now, I wonder how blind I was then. I didn't realize

**The Cult's Tentacles**

the cracks that had begun to form in our lives. We rushed through dinner, left everything on the table—something that had become the norm lately—and hurried out the door. Judy sat in the back seat, chattering away about the upcoming school concert next Friday. Karen and I exchanged a glance, both remembering we had an officers' meeting scheduled for that night. Life had become a constant balancing act, and we were barely keeping up. When we arrived at my parents' house, Judy jumped out first and ran to the door, knocking eagerly. But it stayed shut. She knocked again, more urgently, before my mom finally

**The Cult's Tentacles**

opened it. Her eyes were red, swollen from crying. "You're too late," she said softly, her voice breaking. "He passed about an hour ago. "I froze, the words hitting me like a punch to the gut. I threw my arms around her, and the tears came—tears of guilt, of sorrow, of regret. Karen took Judy back to the car, her sobs muffled in the distance, while I stayed with my mom, holding her as we both cried. "Does Alan know?" I heard Karen ask from behind me. "No," my mom whispered, barely able to speak. Karen went to the phone, dialling quickly. "Alan," she said when someone picked up. "I have bad news. Dad passed away an hour

**The Cult's Tentacles**

ago. "There was silence on the other end, and then Karen hung up. Moments later, the sound of screeching tires echoed down the street. Alan's car came to a halt behind ours. He burst out, eyes wild with grief, and rushed to the door just as Helen climbed out of the passenger seat. She made her way over to Karen, who stood holding Judy, now calmer but still quietly sobbing. Alan saw me sitting beside Dad's bed, holding his cold hand in mine. His face contorted in anger, and he spat the words that pierced my heart. "It's too late now to hold his hand. You should've done it when he was alive But you were too busy with

**The Cult's Tentacles**

that stupid church. "The accusation stung, cutting deep into my soul. I stood up, feeling the weight of his words, but I couldn't respond. I walked over to my mom, rubbing her shoulders gently. Helen came in and took over, comforting her while Karen entered with Judy, who now seemed more composed. She wrapped her arms around her grandmother. "I love you, Grandma," Judy whispered, and the tears started again, flowing freely from all of us. Through it all, Karen remained the calm one, flipping through the phone book for the ambulance number. We waited in silence until they arrived to take Dad

**The Cult's Tentacles**

away. Helen helped my mom gather some clothes; she had already offered to take her home for the night. By the time we got home, it was past midnight. Karen went with Judy to her room, while I stood in the kitchen, staring at the mess we had left behind. She joined me soon after, and we cleaned up together in silence. Once everything was put away, she wrapped her arms around me, holding me close. "I'm so sorry," she whispered. "I'm sorry we weren't there in time to say goodbye." "Yeah," I murmured, my throat tight with unshed tears. "Alan really hurt me tonight. When he saw me holding Dad's hand… he said it was

**The Cult's Tentacles**

too late. He blamed the church for keeping us away. "Karen took my hand, her eyes filled with compassion." Let's go to bed," she said softly, leading me away from the remnants of that heart-breaking night.

As I pulled into the parking lot of the fish and chip shop, a familiar warmth settled over me. It was Friday, our ritual—twelve years strong. The smell of sizzling batter drifted through the evening air, and the little shop glowed like a beacon. The owners greeted me with wide smiles, their faces as familiar as old friends. We had a kind of unspoken bond after all these years.

**The Cult's Tentacles**

Every Friday without fail, I'd be here, collecting our family's weekly takeaway. "Two fish and chips, as usual?" the owner called out cheerfully from behind the counter. "Yes, and don't forget the two red Vienna's," I replied with a grin. "For Judy still doesn't fancy fish much." "Ah yes, can't forget Judy." He chuckled, bagging up the sausages with an extra portion of chips, as he always did. "For our most reliable customer," he winked. It was a small gesture, but it reminded me of the comfort that comes with routines, the sense of belonging in something as simple as ordering takeout. With the warm paper bag in

**The Cult's Tentacles**

hand, I stepped out of the shop. Across the road, the neon sign of the bottle store flickered, stirring a memory. Those old Fridays when I'd pick up a dozen for Kevin. I chuckled quietly to myself. Funny how times change, how some things fade away while others remain like clockwork.

As I drove the short way home, the familiar sight of Judy standing outside, chatting with the neighbours kids, greeted me. The moment she saw the car pull up, her face lit up, and she waved enthusiastically, her excitement contagious. By the time I parked in front of the garage, she was already at

**The Cult's Tentacles**

my side, her arms wrapping around me in a tight hug. "Hello, Dada!" she squealed, her voice full of joy.

"Hello, my princess," I replied, ruffling her hair. She wasted no time, grabbing the takeout bag and darting inside, eager to share the spoils with Karen. She is full of energy, I thought to myself, as I stepped through the front door. The aroma of hot fish and crispy chips filled the house, wrapping me in its embrace. It was a smell that felt like home, like Friday, like the end of the week. "Hi," I greeted Karen as she came over, her smile soft and full of

**The Cult's Tentacles**

something I couldn't quite place. She kissed me, longer than usual, and then she pulled back, her eyes searching mine for a moment. "We need to say a prayer for Dad," she said quietly. "He was cremated at two o'clock this afternoon. Helen called, said the ashes are at their place now." I paused, feeling the weight of her words. "After dinner," I said gently, "we'll say a prayer." Judy had already set the table, the takeout spread across it like a feast. She poured herself a glass of Coke, while Karen and I settled in with coffee. It was a familiar scene—the three of us gathered around, sharing a meal, talking, laughing. There was

**The Cult's Tentacles**

something sacred about these moments, something that made me grateful for the warmth of family, for the simplicity of a meal shared together. I looked around the table, feeling the love that lingered in the air. "We're staying home tonight," I said after a moment. "I'll call the elder later; tell him we won't be at church." Karen reached across the table, her hand resting on mine. Her smile was soft, full of understanding and love. "Thank you," she whispered.

And for a moment, all was quiet. The scent of fish and chips, the warmth of family, the memories of those no

**The Cult's Tentacles**

longer with us—it all mixed together, creating something both bittersweet and beautiful.

Sunday morning, the elder pulled me aside before the service, his eyes narrowing as he asked, "What was Friday all about?" The memory of Friday pierced through my mind. My father had been cremated that afternoon. It wasn't the kind of day one could easily forget. We hadn't gone anywhere, just stayed at home as a family, offering each other what little comfort we could muster. The elder

shifted his tone hardening.
"The dead must bury the dead," he said

**The Cult's Tentacles**

sternly, as if quoting scripture, though none that I could recall. "Make sure that doesn't happen again. An officers' meeting on Friday evening is very important." I nodded, feeling the weight of his disapproval but remaining silent. Inside, though, something stirred. A new voice, perhaps small at first, whispered what I had felt for a while but hadn't dared acknowledge: Family is more important than any church activity. That was the turning point. The first seed of doubt planted itself deep within me, a tiny root curling around my heart. The grip of the church—the unseen but ever-present authority—

**The Cult's Tentacles**

began to feel tighter, suffocating. And for the first time, I felt the urge to resist, pushing back against the tentacles of control that had held me for so long.

After the service, we stood around drinking tea. The usual after-church pleasantries hummed in the air, but I couldn't shake the elder's words. I glanced over at him, sipping from his cup, still surrounded by others who hung on his every word. The tension in my chest flared. Without overthinking, I walked toward him. "This coming Friday," I said my voice surprisingly

**The Cult's Tentacles**

steady, "we won't be at the officers' meeting with the overseer."

His face flushed instantly, his eyes widening in disbelief. "Why not?" he demanded, his voice raised enough to catch the attention of those standing nearby. The subtle conversation around us quieted as people turned, their curiosity piqued. "Don't go anywhere tomorrow evening," he ordered. "I'm coming over. We need to talk."

Now, what most outsiders don't understand about our church is that when an officer above you tells you something, you don't question it. You just do it. Because, as they say, it's not

**The Cult's Tentacles**

just the elder speaking—it's God Himself. Later, after Judy had finished her confirmation class, we greeted some of the other families and walked out to the car. Karen, always observant, glanced at me as we got in.

"Everything alright, John?" she asked, her voice soft but probing "Apparently not," I said, starting the car. "The elder's coming to visit tomorrow evening. We have to stay home. "Yippee!" Judy shouted from the back seat, clearly excited at the thought. Karen smiled faintly, but there was a flicker of concern in her eyes. "Nice,"

**The Cult's Tentacles**

she murmured, though we both knew this was anything but a pleasant visit. I drove home in silence, but inside, my thoughts churned. The elder might think he spoke for God, but for the first time in my life, I wasn't so sure. Family came first. And no elder, no matter how powerful, was going to change that. Monday after work, I rushed home, though the hum of the radio buzzed faintly in the background, I wasn't listening. My thoughts swirled, tugged along by the weight of the day and the looming question: "what does the elder want to talk about?" His request had

**The Cult's Tentacles**

nagged at me since morning, seeping into every corner of my mind like a shadow that wouldn't lift. I gripped the wheel tighter, replaying Alan's words in my head for the hundredth time, his voice still raw with that mix of hurt and anger that only family can cut with. "You should've held Dad's hand when he was alive, not now that he's dead," he had snarled at me. "It's that stupid church that keeps family apart." For the first time, his words had pierced through, landing somewhere deep. And now, as I drove, they throbbed, reverberating through me. He was right, in his own way, about the church—or at least how

**The Cult's Tentacles**

I had let it distance us. *It won't happen again,* I vowed silently. I wouldn't let anything, not tradition, not rituals, keep me from my family again. I was done losing time. As I turned into the driveway, the weight of the day lifted, if only for a moment. Judy, my princess, came bounding toward the car with her infectious smile. "Hello, Dad," she chirped, her arms outstretched as she reached up to kiss me. Her warmth softened the hard edges of my thoughts. "Hey, sweetheart," I murmured, kissing her on the forehead before we walked into the house together. The scent of food hit me first—rich, savoury, familiar.

**The Cult's Tentacles**

My stomach growled in response. Inside, Karen appeared from the kitchen, wiping her hands on a towel, her face lighting up as she kissed me hello. The comforting hum of home settled around me. "Smells amazing in here," I said, as Judy ran ahead to set the table.

"It's dumplings with oxtail," Judy, chimed in, her voice bubbling with excitement." Wow, who made it?" I asked, already knowing the answer but wanting to hear it out loud. "Mom did," Judy grinned. "It's your favourite!" I looked over at Karen, who stood there smiling, a quiet pride

**The Cult's Tentacles**

in her eyes. "This is what matters", I thought, soaking in the moment—the smells, the sounds, the easy rhythm of family life. I walked over to her

Wrapping an arm around her waist. "This is going to be divine," I whispered. For now, at least, everything felt right.

After dinner, Judy helped her mom clean up in the kitchen while I retreated to the lounge, eager to catch up on the latest news. I settled into my armchair, the rustle of the newspaper pages drowning out the gentle clinks And clatters from the kitchen. I was so absorbed in the headlines that I didn't

**The Cult's Tentacles**

notice when a car pulled into the driveway.

From the kitchen, Karen called out, "John, we have visitors." Her voice brought me out of my reverie, and I quickly stood up, realizing the front door had been left ajar. I stepped outside just as the elder greeted me, his voice steady and calm, "Hello, priest." "Hi, elder," I replied, gesturing for him to come in. "Please, come inside."

Karen came out from the kitchen, wiping her hands on a dish towel, and took a seat next to me as I offered my chair to the elder. Judy came from her room to greet him politely, then quietly

**The Cult's Tentacles**

excused herself; slipping back The elder wasted no time. "Priest, I won't take much of your time. I just wanted to understand what's been happening on Friday evenings lately."

I took a breath, carefully choosing my words. "I don't believe there's a problem, elder. Just a series of events. Last Wednesday, my father passed away. I didn't get a chance to say goodbye because I was at breadbreak. He left us while we were at church. By Friday afternoon, he was cremated while I was still at work. We stayed home that evening as a family to offer prayers for him. This coming Friday,

**The Cult's Tentacles**

however, is Judy's year-end concert. We decided we should go. We've already missed one earlier in the year." I paused, hoping my explanation was enough. "So, you see, elder, it's not a problem with Fridays—it's just how things have unfolded." The elder cleared his throat, and when he spoke again, his tone was much gentler than I'd heard from him at the church. "This Friday, the overseer will be leading the meeting, and he insists all officers attend. Why don't you let the sister go with Judy, and you come to the meeting?" I shook my head. "No, elder. I'm going to the school. My family needs me there." His face

**The Cult's Tentacles**

hardened for a moment, and with a sigh, he said, "In that case, I will suspend you until the overseer and I can meet with you." He stood, the weight of his decision settling into the room like a heavy fog.

"That's no problem," I said quietly. "I'll be waiting." He gave a curt nod and made his way out. The door clicked softly behind him, and Karen, who had been holding her breath, broke into a teasing smile. "At least the suspension comes with salary, huh?" I couldn't help but laugh. I picked up one of the scatter cushions and playfully tossed it at her. The tension

**The Cult's Tentacles**

from the evening melted away in our shared laughter, but beneath the surface, I felt it—a twisting, tightening grip of expectation that I was struggling to break free from. Karen's laughter mirrored mine, but deep down, we both knew that this was just the beginning.

It was a cool Wednesday evening, the kind that settles gently after dinner, when we decided to visit Alan. As we pulled up behind his car, the familiar squeak of the brakes announced our arrival. Before Alan could make it to the door, Judy had already flung

**The Cult's Tentacles**

herself forward, wrapping her arms around him in a warm embrace.

"Hello, Uncle Alan!" she chimed, her voice full of the kind of affection only children can muster. Alan smiled that weary but genuine kind of smile, as he hugged her back. His eyes shifted to us, taking in the unexpected visit. "What are you all doing here? You're supposed to be at church," he said, his tone halfway between a greeting and gentle surprise.

"Not tonight," I shrugged, stepping forward to give him a casual shoulder pat. "Where's Mom?" "Inside, with Helen," he answered. Karen leaned in,

**The Cult's Tentacles**

kissed him on the cheek, and without another word, walked into the house like she belonged there—which, in a way, she did. Inside, Mom sat on the worn sofa, looking better than she had in months. The weight of caring for Dad had lifted, and though the grief still lingered in the air, she seemed lighter. Judy was right by her side, holding her hand as if it would anchor them both. "Is Grandma coming Friday to watch the concert?" Judy asked, her voice gentle, but hopeful. Mom smiled, nodding softly. "I'd like to." Judy turned toward Helen. "Aunt Helen, are you coming too? Maybe you and Grandma could drive together." Karen,

**The Cult's Tentacles**

never one to let anything slide, chimed in from the other side of the room. "What about Uncle Alan? Did anyone ask him?" Judy grinned mischievously, her eyes dancing over to Alan. "Please, please?" she pleaded with exaggerated sweetness. Alan looked at Helen, waiting for her cue. Helen just nodded, smiling that soft, sisterly smile. "I wouldn't miss it for the world," Alan said, chuckling. "It'll be a beautiful evening."

As Helen and Karen drifted toward the kitchen, laughter echoing softly in their wake, Judy stayed close to Mom, chatting about little things while I got

**The Cult's Tentacles**

up and made my way to the stoup. Alan followed his footsteps heavy with something unsaid. Outside, under the dim glow of the porch light, the night had fully settled in. The sky was a velvet expanse, and the distant hum of crickets filled the silence between us. Alan's voice broke through, quiet and heavy. "I'm sorry." I didn't ask what for. Instead, I put my arm around his shoulders and pulled him in slightly. "No problem," I said, and for a few minutes, we just stared down the road, the stillness of the night wrapping around us. Then Alan nudged me, motioning with a tilt of his head as he walked toward his garage. The creak of

**The Cult's Tentacles**

the door and the snap of the light switch filled the small space. He pointed to a wooden container, solemn and simple. "Dad's ashes," he said, his voice catching just a little. He cleared his throat and continued. "We're going to bury him on the farm. The new owners are fine with it. "Sunday morning?" I asked. "Yeah. I figured early would be best." "That's fine with me," I said. "We can follow each other. "Karen's voice called out from the house, pulling us back into the warmth of family. We walked back inside, the tension between us gone, replaced by something softer, easier. Karen noticed, giving a quick smile. "Rusks

**The Cult's Tentacles**

are on the table. "We gathered around the kitchen, coffee and rusks in hand. I asked, "What time should we be here Sunday?" "If we can head out early," Alan replied, "we might be back in time for lunch. Then we can have a barbecue." "Sounds great!" Karen beamed, while Helen chimed in. "Eight o'clock Sunday morning works." As the night wound down, and the last few crumbs were brushed away, Judy piped up, her voice reminding us all. "Remember, Friday at seven, the concert starts." We laughed, said our goodbyes, and drove home, the night folding in behind us, peaceful and full of promise.

**The Cult's Tentacles**

Karen had spent the entire week planning. She'd asked Joyce and Kevin to join her at Judy's year-end concert, making sure they understood that it had to be a surprise. For Judy, seeing the entire family there would be a moment to remember, and Karen wasn't going to spoil that by letting it slip early. When she spoke to Joyce, she was firm: "You have to bring our mom too. Judy will never expect the whole family."

They arranged everything down to the last detail. The plan was simple yet exciting—meeting just outside the school before the concert began. No

**The Cult's Tentacles**

fuss, no confusion. It was a time when organizing such things required actual talking, not just a message fired off from a phone screen. There were no cell phones, no personal computers, and certainly no internet to make things easier. A different era. The rich had small black-and-white televisions, but even that felt like a luxury few could afford. The town had its charm though, simpler pleasures like the roadhouse, where families parked their cars to eat, and the drive-in cinema on the outskirts, where entire evenings could be spent under the stars, watching flickering movies on a giant screen. People had telephones, the kind

**The Cult's Tentacles**

with coiled cords that anchored them to the walls of their homes. Fixed, reliable, and familiar, like so much else in those days. Life felt slower, more deliberate.

But as I stood suspended from church, waiting for the elder and overseer, a sense of unease mixed with excitement. The church—well, that was a different story altogether. It looked like a place of comfort and sanctuary, but for us, it now symbolized something else. "False happiness," I whispered under my breath. Just think about what had happened to me. Suspended—my role,

**The Cult's Tentacles**

my identity—stripped away for now, though I knew the church's gaze was still firmly locked on me, watching, waiting. For the first time in a long while, I felt alive. The church's tentacles had loosened their grip on my life, if only briefly. But I wasn't naive the beast still watched from a distance, waiting for its moment. Still, it was a relief to feel that the family's old life had returned, at least for now. Before they'd gotten so involved in the church, things had been simpler, clearer.

Now, even if I was in limbo, Judy's concert was a big deal, especially to

**The Cult's Tentacles**

her neighbours across the road, whose daughter, though younger, attended the same school. Judy and the girl were friendly, often playing together after class. And on the other side, there was Philip, a businessman always on the move, representing his international company. His wife often joined him on his trips abroad, leaving their quiet neighbourhood behind for the bustling cities and far-off places I could only imagine. It was a peaceful area, this little corner of town. We loved it, in spite of everything. There was calm here, a sense of routine. It made us feel that no matter what was happening in our life's, the world continued to turn

**The Cult's Tentacles**

just the same. People came and went, laughed and cried, but in this neighbourhood, things stayed mostly still.

Friday evening had settled over the school, the last rays of sunlight dimming as Judy slipped into the hall, where all the children were bustling about, preparing for the concert. Excitement buzzed in the air, and outside, the ticket queue stretched long and winding, a river of chatter, laughter, and joyful greetings. Old friends reconnected, their voices blending with the crisp autumn breeze.

**The Cult's Tentacles**

We stood outside, tickets already in hand, a small gathering of family and friends waiting for the rest to arrive. Karen, Helen, Alan, Mom, and I formed a little row of eager anticipation, each of us peering down the street for the others. Suddenly, Karen leapt into the air, her hand waving wildly as she spotted them. "They're here!" she cried out, grinning ear to ear.

Joyce, Kevin, and Karen's mom emerged from the crowd, their faces lighting up as they saw us. Kevin was the first to greet me, his grin so wide it was almost comical. "Hello, John!" he

**The Cult's Tentacles**

bellowed, grabbing my hand in an enthusiastic shake that rattled my arm. We laughed, one by one embracing and exchanging cheerful words, the warmth of our shared affection flowing freely. We were all together—a big, boisterous family, talking and laughing.

Karen's mom turned to me with a curious glance. "Weren't you supposed to be at church tonight? It is Friday, after all," she asked, raising an eyebrow. I shrugged, smiling sheepishly. "Suspended until further notice," I said which drew a chorus of laughter from everyone. Kevin,

**The Cult's Tentacles**

standing by Alan, chuckled and added, "Now where have you ever heard of a priest getting suspended?" His tone, paired with the absurdity of the situation, had us all roaring. Just then, the doors to the hall swung open, and we shuffled inside, searching for our row. The place was packed to the brim, the hum of voices echoing off the high ceiling. The atmosphere was like a carnival—colourful, chaotic, alive with anticipation. But as soon as the headmaster appeared on stage, the hall fell into a respectful hush. He read the program with the formality of a well-rehearsed speech, and then disappeared into the wings as the lights dimmed.

**The Cult's Tentacles**

The murmur of excitement grew, only to be silenced when the curtains finally opened. Gasps and murmurs of "ooh" and "aah" rippled through the crowd as the first performers took the stage. Time seemed to fly, and before we knew it, it was Judy's group preparing to perform. As Judy stepped onto the stage, Kevin—always the joker—jumped up and shouted, "Hello, Judy!" His voice boomed through the quiet hall, and the audience erupted in laughter. Judy, mid-step, glanced towards us and saw the whole family sitting in a neat row. A blush crept up her cheeks, but she maintained her composure, ever the professional.

**The Cult's Tentacles**

When the intermission came, the men—me, Alan, and Kevin—headed off to grab drinks for everyone. The cool air outside was a relief, but no sooner had we returned than Judy found us, a wide smile lighting up her face. "I can't believe it!" she exclaimed, practically glowing. "You're all here, my whole family." The joy in her voice was palpable, and her smile was contagious. It was clear the surprise had moved her deeply. The rest of the evening flowed smoothly, filled with more laughter and clapping, the performances a blur of lights and music. By the end, as the crowd filtered out into the night, Karen's

**The Cult's Tentacles**

mom turned to Joyce and whispered, "I think it's time we head home. The evening's getting a bit long for me." We all exchanged our final goodbyes, hugging and promising to meet again soon. As we drove home, Judy's laughter filled the car. "You wouldn't believe it," she said, recounting the moment Kevin had shouted her name. "The kids backstage were teasing me the whole time after that! Every five minutes, they were calling out my name. I think they were jealous—because all of my family was here." She beamed at me, her eyes shining with happiness. I smiled back at her, feeling a quiet warmth settle over me.

**The Cult's Tentacles**

"I'm just glad I could be here," I said softly. It was true. There was nothing quite like family, gathered together, sharing moments like this. And that was worth more than anything.

This Sunday was no time for sleeping in. We were up early, the quiet buzz of the house broken only by the clatter of breakfast. Halfway through my toast, I casually mentioned, "Maybe we should build a bathroom onto our room." Karen glanced up, a knowing smile tugging at her lips. "Why?" she asked, though the mischief in her eyes betrayed her. She already knew where this was going.

**The Cult's Tentacles**

I sighed. "With two women in the house, I'm outnumbered." Before Karen could respond, Judy jumped in, her teenage voice full of playful sarcasm. "Yes! Then Dad can build one onto my room too. That way, Mom won't chase me out again." We all laughed the easy, comfortable kind of laugh that only comes from years of shared jokes. After the kitchen was cleaned and the last of the dishes stacked away, we gathered our things and headed for the car.

The crisp morning air hit us as we stepped outside, waking us up in a way that coffee never could. The sky was

**The Cult's Tentacles**

that pale blue of early morning, a promise of a sunny day ahead. As we pulled out of the driveway, I noticed the newspaper tucked into the post box. "Judy, would you mind?" I asked, slowing down just enough for her to hop out and grab it. We drove down the quiet street towards Alan's house. Today was the day. My father's ashes were finally going to rest on the farm he loved, the place where Alan and I had spent our childhood. It was strange to think that this was the final chapter for him, here, where he had worked, lived, and raised us. Alan's car was already in the road when we arrived, and they were waiting for us,

**The Cult's Tentacles**

engines idling. I nodded to him through the window, and we fell in line, making our way out of town and towards the farm. The city slowly gave way to the open countryside. Judy, ever the city girl, pressed her nose to the window as we passed fields dotted with cows and sheep. "Over there! Is that a sheep? Oh, and cows! So many?" Her excitement was contagious, though my mind drifted to simpler times. Back then, life on the farm was hard work, but it had its charm. We were the kids who smelled like manure at school, the ones who were mocked for wearing the same boots we worked in, but the farm had

**The Cult's Tentacles**

shaped us in ways the city never could. Karen broke my reverie. "I asked Helen to make some picnic sandwiches, and I've packed some cold meats." I turned to her, surprised. "So that's what's in the bag." She smiled. "We wanted it to be a surprise. We're having a picnic under the willow tree, the one you and Alan used to sit under as kids. The owner gave us permission, and he's even had the grass cut." I looked at her, the gratitude welling up in my chest, but all I managed was a soft, "Thank you." Ahead of us, Alan slowed the car, stopping by the gate. Judy asked, "Why's Uncle Alan stopping? "He's opening the gate," I

**The Cult's Tentacles**

said. "It's how we always did it—one of us opened, the other closed. It's tradition." She nodded thoughtfully. "That's nice." As we drove onto the farm, I felt a wave of nostalgia crash over me. The land was different now, but the bones of the place—the rolling fields, the old barns—remained the same. Alan parked under the shade of the willow tree, and I followed suit. We climbed out of the cars and greeted one another properly. Alan gestured to a patch of overgrown grass. "That's where we'll lay him," he said quietly.

A stone lay nearby, worn from years of exposure. The white paint had long

**The Cult's Tentacles**

since faded. "Over here," Alan said, kicking at the dirt a little, marking the spot. While he dug the hole, I grabbed the paintbrush and began repainting the stone. I wanted it to look fresh, like the memory of our father in this place. Judy and the women had already spread out the blanket, unpacking sandwiches and drinks, folding out the chair for Mom.

As Alan's spade hit the earth, he called us over. "Alright, John. You're the priest. Do the honours." I looked at Karen. She gave me a soft, encouraging nod. Clearing my throat, I stepped forward, my heart heavy with

**The Cult's Tentacles**

the weight of the moment. I began the prayer, the words familiar but never easy. "Ashes to ashes, dust to dust," I said, letting a handful of dirt slip through my fingers onto the small box.

When I was done, I stepped back. Alan asked if anyone else wanted to say something, and after a pause, Mom spoke, her voice barely a whisper. "He was a good husband. A good father." Judy stepped forward then, standing close to the grave. "I love you, Grandpa," she whispered, her voice breaking before she ran back to Karen, burying her face in her arms.

**The Cult's Tentacles**

Alan closed the hole, packing the dirt with his boot, and I placed the freshly painted stone on top. As we slowly walked back to the picnic blanket, I carried the paint back to Alan's car. Let me put it in he said, opening the trunk. We spent the rest of the afternoon sitting under that willow tree, just like we had as kids. My mind wandered back to those Sundays from years ago, when it was Mom, Dad, Alan, and me, sharing sandwiches and ginger beer under the same branches. Life, it seemed, had come a full circle.

**The Cult's Tentacles**

That evening, back at home, I found myself sinking into the worn, familiar cushions of the lounge, the scent of freshly brewed coffee wafting through the room. The Sunday paper lay open in my lap, but it was hard to focus. Judy had been talking non-stop about the farm since we got back, her excitement spilling over into every word. "Why don't you buy a farm, Dad?" she asked suddenly, her eyes wide with curiosity and hope.

I lowered the paper and looked at her. "To do what?" I asked, more amused than serious. "To have lots of animals!" she answered, her voice

**The Cult's Tentacles**

bubbling with enthusiasm as she began to list off every creature she could think of. From cows to chickens, and even a donkey. The words came fast, as if she could already see the fields filled with her imagined menagerie.

Karen, sitting nearby, smiled softly, that knowing look on her face. "You know," she said, her voice steady, "we could've bought that same farm once. We wanted to. But back then, we didn't have the money." Her words hung in the air for a moment, as if the memory lingered between us. Judy, ever the realist in her innocent way tilted her head. "Do we have money

**The Cult's Tentacles**

now?" I shook my head with a quiet chuckle. "Not exactly," I began, but before I could continue, the shrill ring of the phone cut through the room. Judy leapt from her chair and darted to the hallway. "Hello?" she answered, "Yes, fine, thank you. Oh, yes, he's here. Dad, it's for you." With a sigh, I rose and walked over, taking the receiver from her. "Hello?" I said, unsure who'd be calling at this hour. "It's the elder," a familiar voice greeted me. "How are you?" "Fine, fine," I replied. "What can I do for you?" "Listen," the elder continued, "we're coming to see you tomorrow evening. Me and the overseer. We need to talk."

**The Cult's Tentacles**

I paused for a moment, a flicker of surprise crossing my mind. "No problem," I said, forcing ease into my voice. "I'll see you both tomorrow, then."

As I hung up and turned back, Karen was watching me closely, as if she could already guess the news. "The elder?" she asked. "Yep," I confirmed, walking back to my seat. "He and the overseer are coming tomorrow evening." A grin broke across Karen's face. "Maybe you should ask them for an extension on your suspension," she teased, and in that instant, the whole room erupted into laughter, the kind

**The Cult's Tentacles**

that lingers after long days of sun and talk of dreams. Judy stood up, stretching her arms and yawning. She kissed both Karen and me on the cheek, her goodnight kiss warm and full of affection. "I'm going to bed early," she said. "Goodnight, Dad. Goodnight, Mom." As she walk away, Karen must have caught the look on my face—the trace of worry, maybe a little fatigue—because she stood and walked over, her hands resting gently on my shoulders. She leaned in and kissed me softly. "Don't worry," she whispered. "It'll all work out. Let's turn in early too. After a whole day out on that farm, I'm exhausted." I smiled

**The Cult's Tentacles**

at her, grateful. Together, we stood and made our way to the bedroom, the lights of the house fading into darkness behind us, the last embers of the day still glowing faintly in our minds. Tomorrow would come soon enough, but for tonight, there was peace.

Monday afternoons were always quiet, but today felt different. I was just coming home from work, and as I turned the corner toward our house, I saw Judy walking by the gate, her ponytail bouncing with each step. She didn't see me at first, but as I pulled into the driveway, she turned away from the front door and came to greet

**The Cult's Tentacles**

me with a warm smile. "Hello, Dad," she said, her voice bright as ever. "Where've you been?" I asked, kissing her forehead. "Oh, I went to Sylvia's to give her a program," she said nonchalantly, brushing a strand of hair behind her ear. "A program?" I raised an eyebrow. "Yep, from Friday's concert," she replied. "Ah," I nodded, letting it go as we walked inside together. But just as we stepped in, an odd smell hit me, something sharp, almost acrid.

Karen appeared from the bedroom, her expression sheepish. "John, I burned the food," she admitted, running a hand

**The Cult's Tentacles**

through her hair. "Mom called, Judy was across the street, and I just... I forgot it was in the oven." I smiled, pulling her close for a kiss. "No problem. It was an accident," I said, brushing it off. "How about tuna sandwiches instead?" She looked up at me, her eyes full of relief. "Is that okay?"

"Anything you make tastes great," I reassured her. Her face lit up with a smile, and Judy, who had overheard, piped in from the kitchen. "Can I have peanut butter instead? You know I hate fish." Karen laughed, rolling her eyes playfully. "Fine, fine. Come help me,

**The Cult's Tentacles**

Judy." I settled into my favourite chair, the scent of burnt food already fading into the background. And started flipping through the business section. One headline immediately caught my attention, and I couldn't help but let out a low whistle. Karen, busy in the kitchen, looked over her shoulder. "Any good news?" she asked, half-curious." Come take a look," I said, folding the paper to show her. She wiped her hands on a towel and wandered over, glancing at the article. "What am I supposed to see?" she asked, squinting slightly. "The map," I pointed, tapping the page. "The mine's buying out all the farms in this area—

**The Cult's Tentacles**

right where Dad's farm was." Her eyebrows shot up. "Is that good news or bad news?" she asked, leaning on the table. "Well, if we'd bought the farm from Dad when we had the chance, we'd be looking at three times our investment right now," I said with a shake of my head. Karen just sighed, heading back to the kitchen to pour coffee. "Come on, sit down. Sandwiches are almost ready," she called over her shoulder.

We ate together, and Judy chattered happily about how the teachers had been thrilled with the concert's success. "The kids jump up and shout

**The Cult's Tentacles**

my name when they see me," she giggled, and we all laughed. It was good to see her so happy. "Uncle Kevin's always unpredictable at events like these," Karen remarked, shaking her head with a fond smile. "You never know what to expect."

After dinner, while the two of them cleaned up, I went to the phone to call Alan. The news about the farms had been bothering me, and I needed to talk it over with someone who'd understand. After a few minutes of small talk, I finally got to the point. "Alan, did you hear the mine's buying up all the land around Dad's old farm?

**The Cult's Tentacles**

"He let out a low whistle, much like I had earlier. "No kidding. That's big news." As we talked, a pair of headlights cut across the driveway, drawing my attention. "Look, I've got to go. The elders are here," I said, cutting the conversation short. Alan understood, and we hung up. Karen was rushing around the kitchen, putting away the last of the dishes when I opened the door. "Hello, Overseer. Hello, Elder," I greeted them, stepping aside to let them in. Judy came in to greet them too, exchanging pleasantries before excusing herself to her room. Karen joined us in the living room, sitting

**The Cult's Tentacles**

close beside me, her hand resting lightly on mine. The overseer was the first to speak. "Did you enjoy the concert?" he asked his tone friendly enough. "I did, yes," I replied, feeling a slight tension in the air. He leaned forward, his eyes narrowing just slightly. "There seems to be a misunderstanding about your situation. "A misunderstanding?" I asked my brow furrowing.

"It seems you don't fully understand how things work in the church," he continued, his voice calm but with an undercurrent of something heavier. "All worldly activities… they are

**The Cult's Tentacles**

against the spirit. The church's activities—that is where the spirit lies. That's how we serve God, in spirit and truth. Do you understand?" Karen squeezed my hand. I could feel her tension matching my own. "I think so," I said cautiously.

The overseer shook his head, clearly not satisfied. "If you did, you would've been at the officers' meeting," he said, his eyes on both of us, lingering on Karen. I cleared my throat. "Have you ever seen a body walk around without a head?" I asked him, knowing where this conversation was going. The overseer's smile didn't waver. "Why

**The Cult's Tentacles**

do you ask?" he replied, already knowing the answer.

"Because the man is the head of the woman, just as the woman is over the child," I said firmly, but before I could say more, the elder interrupted. "It's not the same," he said, his voice sharp. "Brothers," the overseer cut in smoothly, "let's take it easy. You're right, priest, you are the head of your family, but," he added with a sly smile, "in the spirit."

"Why did you really come tonight, Overseer?" I asked, cutting through the tension. "To see what you understand," he said, standing up slowly. "And from

**The Cult's Tentacles**

tomorrow evening, you must be in your place." Karen, ever the host, offered them something to drink, but they declined politely, mentioning another appointment. They left soon after, all smiles and handshakes, but the unease in the room lingered long after I locked the door behind them. I stood there for a moment, thinking. The tentacles of the beast were getting tighter, squeezing the daylight out of me.

Life had a way of settling into its own rhythm, like the predictable sway of the tides. Church, work, sleep—it all folded into a seamless routine, the days

**The Cult's Tentacles**

bleeding into one another until the seasons changed and we found ourselves nearing the end of yet another year. The urgency to gather new members into the church swelled in our hearts each December, as it always did. It had become more than a mission—it was our life.

Family gatherings, once the heartbeat of our weekends, grew less frequent. Judy, our daughter, had gone off to university, fully immersed in her studies to become a teacher. It seemed like only yesterday she was running through the church hallways, her laughter bouncing off the old walls.

**The Cult's Tentacles**

Now, she was building a life of her own, as all children eventually do.

For me, a shift had come in my spiritual walk. I had been ordained as an elder, a position I never aspired to but one that felt like a natural culmination of the years spent in quiet service. The previous elder had taken on a greater role, now regarded as our prophet, a figure of reverence in the congregation. And in many ways, we were content—if not fulfilled, at least at peace.

Both of our mothers had passed on in recent years, their absence felt like an ever-present shadow lingering over

**The Cult's Tentacles**

family gatherings. It was as if, with their passing, the glue that held us all together had loosened. Alan and Helen had moved to Cape Town. Distance now separated us, both physically and emotionally. We heard from them less and less.

But life, in its peculiar way, offered compensations. Kevin, my brother-in-law, had found an unexpected fortune after his boss passed away. He bought the workshop, stepping into a new role as its owner. It was strange seeing him wear that mantle of responsibility, a man who had always been more comfortable in the background. There

**The Cult's Tentacles**

was one constant, though—Joyce. Karen's sister. She still visited some mornings, her presence a quiet reassurance in our otherwise shifting world. She would sit with Karen, sipping tea, the two of them talking in low murmurs about the past, the future, and everything in between. They didn't need many words—there was something about their bond that went beyond conversation. Yes, in many ways, life seemed perfect. We had everything we needed, or so we thought. Even at work, things remained much the same after Mr.JP the boss, passed on. His son had taken over, and although he shared his father's initials,

**The Cult's Tentacles**

there were subtle changes. We had moved on from the old ways, now working with PC's instead of filing cabinets. It was progress, of course, but it was strange how quickly the familiar faded. Looking back, it was a quiet contentment that we lived in—a peace that only comes before the storm. At the time, we didn't see the small cracks in our carefully constructed lives, or perhaps we simply chose not to. After all, it was easier to believe that everything was perfect, even when, deep down, we knew that life had a way of changing when you least expected it.

**The Cult's Tentacles**

It was a quiet Friday afternoon at work, the kind where time seems to stretch a little longer, and I found myself with a rare moment of free time. The office was unusually still, the hum of the old desktop computer in front of me becoming the only sound that broke the silence. With a few minutes to spare, I decided to embark on a search I had been meaning to do for some time: the origins of our church.

Now, I should mention, this was before Google had become a household name. We didn't have the luxury of endless information at our fingertips. Back then, we used Wandex, a rudimentary

**The Cult's Tentacles**

search engine that paled in comparison to anything available today. It was even before the days of Yahoo. The results were slow, often incomplete, but I was determined to dig into the history that had always intrigued me.

What I uncovered that day was far from anything I could have ever imagined. For years, we had been taught that our church's foundation traced back to the apostles of the Bible, its roots divinely planted in ancient times. It was ingrained in us like a sacred truth. But what I found that afternoon shattered that illusion. The apostle who had supposedly started our

**The Cult's Tentacles**

church hadn't been connected to the Bible at all—he had been excommunicated from a previous church, one with its origins in the UK. That church, after moving its base to Germany, sent an apostle to Australia to oversee matters on behalf of the Germans. That apostle, in turn, dispatched a man to South Africa, tasked with establishing the apostolic presence in Africa. I leaned closer to the screen, heart pounding as I read. That man, the one sent to South Africa, was later called back to Australia and ordained as an apostle for Africa. But that's where the story took an unexpected turn. After breaking away

**The Cult's Tentacles**

from the German church, he formed his own splinter group, a church of his own making. He ignored the directives from Germany, did his own thing, and Germany, in response, ordained a new apostle for South Africa while excommunicating the original one. A lawsuit ensued, the Germans accusing him of continuing to use their name even after being cut off. The whole affair was a tangled mess of power struggles and deceit. But the real shock, the blow that landed deep in my chest, was this: the church I had believed in, the one I had so proudly been a part of, was built on a lie. It wasn't a continuation of the Bible's

**The Cult's Tentacles**

apostles. It was the creation of a man who had been cast out, a man who had started a church of his own design, under false pretences.

I sat back in my chair, stunned. My mind raced through the years of belief, the sermons I had attended, the teachings I had shared with others. How many people had I unknowingly misled, passing on a legacy I believed to be divine, only to discover it was rooted in deception? It was as though the ground had shifted beneath me.

Driving home later that day, the streets blurred as I struggled to process what I had just uncovered. The familiar

**The Cult's Tentacles**

landmarks of the town felt strange, distant, like I was seeing them for the first time. I was still reeling from the revelation when I passed the fish and chips shop, realizing too late that Karen had asked for dinner. The weight of the day's discovery was heavy, but I couldn't return home empty-handed. I pulled a U-turn, heart still pounding, and headed back to the shop. Karen was expecting fish and chips tonight, and I couldn't fail her, not after everything else. As I waited for my order, my thoughts swirled. How long had I been lied to? How many times had I repeated those lies, unaware of the truth? This, I realized,

**The Cult's Tentacles**

was the beginning of something much larger—an unravelling of all the tightly bound threads of faith and tradition that had held me captive for so long. That day marked the first crack in the foundation of a belief system that I had never thought to question. It was the start of me pushing back, slowly but surely, against the tentacles of a faith that had, for all these years, held me tightly in its grasp. Arriving home, I barely had time to turn off the engine before I saw Karen standing in the doorway, as if she had heard the car before it even touched the driveway. She was smiling, and I

**The Cult's Tentacles**

couldn't help but smile back as I climbed out of the car, the evening air crisp around us. We exchanged a quick kiss, familiar and warm, before she turned back inside, the bag of fish and chips already in her hand.

I stepped in after her, noticing the newspaper lying on my seat in the lounge, just as it always had been for years. Judy, ever since she could remember, had been the one to fetch it from the post box the moment it arrived, leaving it there for me before heading off to her day. Now that she was off at varsity, it was Karen who'd taken over the little ritual, a subtle shift

**The Cult's Tentacles**

that reminded me how much time had passed. It wasn't a big thing, but it struck me in a way that felt deeper than it should have. I walked into the kitchen, the familiar smell of fried fish and vinegar filling the house. Karen had already poured us coffee, and we sat down together, the silence comfortable until she finally spoke. "Everything alright at work?" she asked, her eyes searching mine. "Yeah, everything's fine," I replied, but even I could hear the hesitation in my voice. Karen knew me too well, and I wasn't fooling her.

**The Cult's Tentacles**

She tilted her head, waiting, and I sighed, running a hand through my hair. "It's just... something I found out today. About the church." I began, my voice low as I explained, laying it all out for her, detail by detail. The lies. The deception I had uncovered. The foundation of the very institution I had trusted for so long, crumbling in front of me. Karen didn't say a word as I spoke, but her jaw literally dropped at one point, and when I was finished, she sat back, shaking her head in disbelief. "Are you sure?" she asked, her voice quiet. I nodded. "One hundred per cent." She exhaled her eyes distant for a moment as she processed everything.

**The Cult's Tentacles**

But then, as if to ground herself again, she switched topics. "Judy called today," she said softly. "She's coming home next Wednesday. And we'll need to be back for her graduation on Friday."

I felt my chest tighten at that. Our little girl, done with her studies already, moving into the world. "She's already applied for a few teaching posts," Karen continued, squeezing my hand. "Can you believe it? We're that old." "Maybe I should see if I can get her a job at the company," I joked, though part of me felt the weight of time more heavily than I let on.

**The Cult's Tentacles**

Karen gave me a look. "She studied to be a teacher, remember?" "Alright, you win," I said, laughing lightly. She always won these little exchanges. She smiled before continuing. "Joyce was here this morning, by the way. She's going to help Kevin full-time in the workshop starting next month. He's struggling with the paperwork, poor thing." I chuckled at that, knowing full well how Kevin battled with anything administrative. "That's understandable," I said. With that, I excused myself to the lounge, where my newspaper waited. I had just settled into the couch when Karen's voice called from the kitchen, reminding me

**The Cult's Tentacles**

of tonight's meeting with the priests. "Do I have to go?" I called back, not really wanting to face them after what I had learned. "You're their elder," she reminded me, though I could tell from her tone she knew how much I was dreading it. "Not for long," I muttered under my breath, a little louder than I'd meant to. "What was that?" Karen asked. "Nothing, just talking to myself," I said quickly. She laughed from the kitchen. "You're getting old." I smiled, shaking my head, but deep down, her words hit a little closer to home than I would have liked.

**The Cult's Tentacles**

First, I said, "Tell me everything." Judy glanced at her mom, fingers fiddling nervously in her lap. "Well," she began hesitantly, "there's this guy." Karen and I exchanged glances, both of us fighting smiles. Before I could stop her, Karen leaned in, teasing, "Which guy?" "Mom, please," Judy sighed, clearly flustered. "Let me finish." She paused, gathering her thoughts, and continued, "He's someone who studied with me. He's graduating on Friday too." "Oh," I said, raising an eyebrow. "Was he the only guy in your course?" "Dad, please," Judy replied with an exasperated look. "Can I just talk?" John, my inner voice

**The Cult's Tentacles**

warned, plays it cool. Karen, ever the voice of calm, gently urged, "Go ahead, darling. We won't interrupt." Judy took a breath, steadying herself. "His name is Trevor." I gave a brief nod, our eyes meeting as she spoke. She went on, "At the beginning of the year, we officially started going out—like, seriously." I could feel the room shift. The light-hearted air that had surrounded us only moments ago had grown heavier, more serious. "You'll meet him and his parents on Friday," Judy continued. "They'll be at the graduation, too." I stared straight ahead, not quite sure what to say. Karen, sensing my hesitation, stepped

**The Cult's Tentacles**

in. "So, what about him?" she asked, her voice calm but curious. Judy swallowed, clearly working up the courage to drop the bigger news. "Trevor wants to come over after the ceremony... to properly meet you both. And..." she hesitated, her voice dropping a bit, "to ask for my hand." Karen's eyes widened and I could see the faintest tremor of worry flicker across her face. "Are you sure?" she asked softly. Judy nodded, more confidently this time. "We've talked about it. We're going to get engaged for a year first. Then we'll decide when to get married." I finally found my voice. "When's the big day?" I asked,

**The Cult's Tentacles**

trying to keep my tone neutral. "I'm not sure," Judy admitted. "We want to take our time, get engaged first, and then see how things go."

Karen, ever the practical one, chimed in again. "And what do his parents think?" "Trevor says they won't have a problem with it," Judy assured us. There was a pause, the weight of everything hanging in the air. Then, as if to break the tension, Judy got up, walked over to me, and wrapped her arms around my shoulders. "I'll always love you, Dad," she said, her voice softer now.

**The Cult's Tentacles**

I hugged her back, the moment sinking in as I realized that my little girl was no longer that. She kissed me quickly on the cheek before moving to her mother. "Mom, don't worry," she said, her voice filled with reassurance. "Everything will work out." She kissed Karen too, then sat back down, waiting for a response. Karen and I exchanged another glance, this one more serious. "Alright," I said finally. "Let's wait until Friday and see how it goes." Then, as if snapping back into my usual self, I asked, "Where's he going to sleep?" "In the lounge," Judy said matter-of-factly. "I'll make up a bed for him." I couldn't resist. "Why not

**The Cult's Tentacles**

the garage?" I teased, trying to lighten the mood again. Judy gave me a playful shove, laughing. "Dad, he won't mind." With the heaviness lifted, we all started laughing together. Karen stood up, her voice back to its usual lightness. "Who wants coffee?" "Of course," I replied. "Make mine strong. I' need it." As they headed to the kitchen, I sat back and watched them, especially Judy. For the first time, I truly saw her—no longer my little girl, but a young woman, ready to take on the world.

**The Cult's Tentacles**

Thursday was a day like any other at the office. The routine had become so ingrained that it felt like I could do it in my sleep: emails, reports, numbers, always and numbers. By noon, I decided it was time to see the boss. There was something I needed to ask, something important. Climbing the stairs to his office, my mind wandered. I thought of Judy, my daughter, and her graduation tomorrow. How time flies.

The P.A. was at her desk when I reached the top. "Is Mr JP busy?" I asked, standing a bit nervously by her desk. "Just a moment," she replied

**The Cult's Tentacles**

with a practiced smile. She picked up the phone and spoke in a low tone. "John's here to see you." As she set the receiver down, she looked up. "You can go in." I took a deep breath and opened the door, closing it softly behind me. Mr JP sat behind his polished oak desk, the sunlight from the window casting long shadows across the room. "Morning, John," he greeted me with an easy smile. Much more approachable than his father had ever been. I'd been with the company long enough to know the difference. His father had ruled with an iron fist, but this new boss—he was different, more modern in his approach. "Sir," I

**The Cult's Tentacles**

began, not wasting time, "Judy's graduation is tomorrow, and I'd like to—" "Sure," he cut in, without hesitation. "You can have the day off." I blinked. That was easier than I expected. "Does she have a job lined up? Or has she applied anywhere?" he asked, leaning back in his chair, arms crossed. "Yes, sir. She's applied to a few teaching posts," I replied. I could barely get the words out before he was off again. "Teaching? Doesn't she know she can make more money in finance?" he said, raising an eyebrow. "There's good money in numbers."

**The Cult's Tentacles**

I smiled slightly. "I think teaching is what she's passionate about, sir. She's also getting engaged on Friday—to someone she studied with." "Ah," he said, his voice softening for a moment. "And what about him? Does he want a career in finance?" I shrugged. "I'm not sure. They've both got their own paths." "If he needs a job, tell him to come see me," Mr JP offered. "We need young people in the firm, people to take us to the next level. Who's going to teach the next generation when you and Phil retire, hmm?" I stiffened at that word. Retire. It hadn't even crossed my mind, not seriously, anyway. "Do you realize there are

**The Cult's Tentacles**

twelve people in this company set to retire in the next fifteen to twenty years?" he continued. "We need replacements—people who know this place inside and out. People like you." He smiled, but the weight of his words lingered.

"Enjoy the kids while you've still got them, John," he said, his tone warm as he nodded toward the door. I muttered my thanks and left his office, my thoughts in a whirl. Retirement? It felt... unfair. I loved my work. I loved the satisfaction of balancing figures, of making sense out of chaos. It was who I was, part of my identity. I wasn't

**The Cult's Tentacles**

ready to give that up. But then, as I descended the staircase, I smiled to myself. At least the boss wasn't going to push me out before my time. That was some comfort. Besides, tomorrow was Judy's day, and that was what mattered most right now.

Friday afternoon had a golden glow to it, the kind that warmed the heart and softened the edges of everything, even the wait as the photographer wrapped up the graduation photo shoot. It was a day we had dreamed of for years—Judy, our daughter, had finally received her degree. Pride bubbled up inside me as I watched her and a young

**The Cult's Tentacles**

man standing side by side, degrees in hand, grinning at the camera. The photographer scribbled down our mailing address before Judy and the young man made their way toward us. "Mom, Dad," she said, her voice carrying a note of excitement, "this is Trevor." We greeted him warmly, exchanging firm handshakes. Trevor, polite but nervous, excused himself after a moment and vanished into the sea of graduates and their families. A few minutes later, he reappeared, this time with a man and a woman. "Mom, Dad," he introduced them with a smile, "this is my mom, Lulu, and my dad, Chris." We shook hands, introducing

**The Cult's Tentacles**

ourselves to Trevor's parents, making small talk about the ceremony and how relieved we were for our children to finally be done with their studies. They were lovely people, from the other side of Potchefstroom, while we hailed from Carletonville. Time passed easily in conversation, though they eventually excused themselves, explaining their younger children were waiting at home. As they left, Judy turned to us, her face beaming. "Thank you for coming and sharing this day with us. Trevor and I are heading out with the class for milkshakes at the roadhouse." Before I could say a word, Karen, my wife, chimed in with a nod and a smile.

**The Cult's Tentacles**

"That's fine, you two go ahead. Come on, John, let's get home."

Karen had prepared one of her famous pasta dishes for dinner, and the smell welcomed us the moment we walked through the door. Not long after we'd settled in, the sound of a car pulling into the driveway reached us. Judy and Trevor had arrived in his old VW Beetle, their smiles as bright as their graduation gowns, which they still hadn't taken off.

At the dinner table, we were just about to dig in when the phone rang. Karen stood, wiping her hands on her apron as she answered. "Hello? Fine, thank

**The Cult's Tentacles**

you… yes, he's here." She turned toward me, her face slightly tense. "John, it's the overseer. Sighing, I took the phone. "Hello, overseer," I greeted him. "Elder," his voice came through the line, sharp and impatient, "why aren't you at the prophet's house? You were expected."

I felt a sudden tension rise in my chest. "We were in Potchefstroom for Judy's graduation," I explained. "She received her degree today, and we just got home. We're about to—" But before I could finish, the line went dead. I stared at the receiver for a moment before hanging up. Karen sensed

**The Cult's Tentacles**

something was off, but she said nothing as we continued with dinner. Judy, still glowing with happiness, sat close to Trevor, her hand resting lightly on his arm. He seemed content, quietly enjoying his meal.

After we finished eating, I motioned to Trevor. "Let's sit in the lounge," I suggested, "while the women clean up." He followed me, and once we were settled, I asked, "So, have you applied for any jobs yet?" "Yes, Uncle John," he replied, respectful as ever. "I've applied to a few places—Pretoria, East London, and Fochville." "Mmm," I nodded.

**The Cult's Tentacles**

"Teaching doesn't pay all that well, does it?" "It depends on the school," he said, a little uncertain. "Well, have you thought about JPK Auditors? They're looking for junior financial managers. The starting salaries about the same as a teacher's, but you don't have to work weekends, and you'll get paid over the December break when the company closes. If you love working with figures, you might be able to start as early as next week."

Trevor's eyes lit up. "Really? Where are they based?" "If you're here Monday morning at 7:30, I'll take you there," I said, smiling. "You never

**The Cult's Tentacles**

know, opportunities like this don't come around often." His face broke into a wide grin. "Thank you, Uncle John. Wow. "As we sat there, the women joined us, and Trevor was still smiling ear to ear. Judy noticed. "What's got you smiling like that?" she asked, her tone teasing.

"Your dad's taking me to JPK on Monday! I might start working right away—and I'll get paid in December when they close!" Judy gave an exaggerated sigh and grinned. "Let me guess, JPK Auditors?" Trevor's eyes widened in surprise. "How did you know?" "Because my dad works

**The Cult's Tentacles**

there," she laughed, and soon, we were all laughing. Our laughter was interrupted by the sound of another car pulling into the driveway. It was the overseer and the evangelist. Karen, ever the gracious hostess, greeted them, though I noticed the tension in her smile. She suggested, after the greetings, that Judy and Trevor head to her room. They did so obediently, leaving us to the inevitable conversation. The overseer wasted no time. "Elder," he began, his voice hard, "this is becoming a pattern. You've become too big in yourself, thinking you don't need permission to miss a gathering."

**The Cult's Tentacles**

I looked him straight in the eye. "This was my daughter's graduation. A once-in-a-lifetime event. I don't regret attending it." The evangelist, his voice low and rumbling, chimed in. "You should've asked the prophet for permission." "I don't need anyone's permission to celebrate my daughter's achievements," I replied, my tone firmer now. Karen squeezed my hand, a silent reminder to keep calm.

The overseer, clearly agitated, stood. "I'm going to speak to the apostle about this." I shrugged, a small smile playing on my lips. "Feel free to call him from here, if you like. "The

**The Cult's Tentacles**

evangelist shook his head. "That won't be necessary," he muttered, and with a curt farewell, they left. As the door closed behind them, Karen looked at me with a relieved smile. "Thank you," she whispered, and I knew it wasn't just for the words I'd spoken, but for standing firm for our family.

It was a bright Saturday morning, and after breakfast, the women left to do some shopping, preparing for the afternoon's barbecue. She had salads in mind and a list of things to gather. Meanwhile, I turned to Trevor, tapping his shoulder lightly. "Trevor, would you mind driving me to Kevin's in your

**The Cult's Tentacles**

Beetle?" I asked. He raised an eyebrow. "Who's Kevin?"

A grin spread across my face. "Uncle John," I replied mysteriously, enjoying the curiosity in his eyes. "You'll see." Trevor agreed, and as we drove, I directed him through familiar streets, passing by old landmarks, eventually reaching Kevin's workshop. As soon as we pulled up, Kevin, who had spotted the Beetle from afar, came over with his usual broad grin. His face lit up when he saw me. "Howzit!" he

hollered, his voice full of that unmistakable energy. "Hi, Kev!" I greeted, stepping out of the car and

**The Cult's Tentacles**

walking over to him. Kevin's eyes then shifted toward Trevor, taking him in. "This is Trevor," I explained, patting Trevor on the back. "He and Judy are getting engaged this afternoon, and Karen's supposed to give you a call about it." Kevin's face brightened even more, and he reached out to shake Trevor's hand with such enthusiasm that Trevor's eyes grew wide in surprise. "Congratulations, Trevor!" Kevin said with a firm handshake, almost knocking the breath out of him. "Thanks," Trevor mumbled, still wide-eyed. "By the way," I added, "could you take a look at the Beetle? Maybe give it a quick service? Trevor's going

**The Cult's Tentacles**

to need it in tip-top shape for today." Before Trevor could object, I held up a hand. "Don't worry, I'll cover the cost."

A shy smile tugged at Trevor's lips as Kevin called over one of his mechanics, a burly man covered in grease, but with kind eyes. "This guy's the best man for the job," Kevin said confidently. "Give him the keys." Trevor hesitated but handed them over. With that, Kevin motioned for us to follow him inside the workshop. The office was surprisingly neat. Papers were stacked neatly on the desk, and a radio played rock music a little too

**The Cult's Tentacles**

loudly from the corner. I raised an eyebrow, gesturing at the clean space. "And this?" I asked, curious. "Joyce," Kevin said with a chuckle. "She comes in every day to help me with the admin work." Kevin headed over to the small fridge and pulled out a beer. "Would you like one?" he asked Trevor. "No, thanks," Trevor replied politely. "I'll just have a Coke." Kevin grinned, handing Trevor a bottle of Coke and tossing me a cheeky look. "John here is a priest, so I'll spare him the temptation." I laughed and took a seat across from Kevin, who cracked open his beer. We chatted for a while, catching up, when suddenly Kevin

**The Cult's Tentacles**

turned to Trevor, his eyes glinting with an idea. "Trevor, why don't you become an appy?" Trevor blinked. "A what?" "An apprentice, of course!" Kevin said with a laugh. "Mechanic—then you can service your own car."

We all burst out laughing, imagining Trevor tinkering under the hood of a car. But Trevor quickly shook his head. "No, no," I interrupted with a chuckle. "Trevor's going to work at JPK." Kevin whistled, shaking his head with mock disapproval. "Ah, so you want to be a paper mechanic, huh?" The laughter continued until Kevin suggested we check on the car.

**The Cult's Tentacles**

We walked back to the workshop, where Trevor's Beetle was still up on the ramp.

"Just checking the brakes," one of the mechanics called out. "Almost done." We stepped outside into the warm sunshine, stretching our legs a bit. Kevin sighed contentedly, looking around his workshop. "Man, I'm glad I bought this place nine years ago," he said. "Time flies," I mused, thinking back. Just then, we heard a car horn. The mechanic waved us over, and Kevin grinned. "Your jalopy's ready to go. A1 condition!"

**The Cult's Tentacles**

I smiled, patting Kevin's shoulder. "I'll make things right on Monday," he said, waving us off. "See you later—and should I bring my own beer?" I laughed as we got back into the Beetle. As we started driving, I nudged Trevor, seeing the thought on his face. "You should stop at the filling station," I told him. Trevor opened his mouth to speak, but I cut him off with a grin. "How are you going to get to work on an empty tank?"

While the car was being filled, Trevor turned to me, a soft gratitude in his voice. "Thank you, Uncle John." "Don't worry, kiddo," I said, giving

**The Cult's Tentacles**

him a reassuring smile. "Just be here on Monday." And with that, we drove home, ready for the day's festivities.

The afternoon had unfolded into a perfect family barbecue, the kind of gathering where everything just clicks. The smoky aroma of sizzling meat filled the backyard, mingling with the warm breeze, while soft music played in the background, blending with the laughter and chatter of family. Even Kevin, usually the loud one, was surprisingly quiet. Maybe we were all just getting older, settling into the calmness of the day.

**The Cult's Tentacles**

Plates piled high; everyone was busy enjoying the food when Judy stood up to turn off the radio. A sudden hush fell over the group, as if the moment itself was holding its breath. Then Trevor, standing in the centre, cleared his throat and began to speak. "Everybody, I just want to say a huge thank you to Aunt Karen and Uncle John for giving us their blessing... to get engaged."

A ripple of surprise went through the crowd. But before anyone could react, Kevin broke the silence, his voice sharp but playful. "We didn't give you permission!" he joked, grinning

**The Cult's Tentacles**

widely. Joyce, ever the peacemaker, scolded, "Kevin, quiet!" But the smile on her face betrayed her amusement. Judy moved to stand beside Trevor, her cheeks flushed with excitement.
"Mom, Dad," she began, her voice soft but clear, "we love each other, and we just wanted to thank you both." Trevor, beaming with pride, gently took Judy's hand and slipped a delicate ring onto her finger. The women in the family clapped with joy, and Karen, seated nearby, couldn't hold back a tear that slid down her cheek. I nodded, fighting the lump in my throat, feeling my own eyes sting. My little girl, my Judy, was glowing with happiness. Before I knew

**The Cult's Tentacles**

it, Kevin had raised his beer, laughing. "Cheers! May you have plenty of kids?" "They're not married yet!" Joyce shouted back, and we all laughed along. The warmth of the moment filled every corner of the yard. I finally found my voice, "Congratulations, Judy. "Who came over to me, her eyes sparkling as she wrapped her arms around me in a hug. "Thank you, Dad," she whispered, her words just for me. She moved to Karen next, sharing a quiet moment with her mother, before Trevor came over, hand extended. "Thank you, Uncle John," he said, his gratitude genuine. Before long, the chatter picked back up, the music

**The Cult's Tentacles**

playing softly once again in the background. Kevin, beer in hand, gave me a hearty handshake, leaning in to mutter, "Congratulations, man." And just like that, I stood there, feeling the weight of the day and the happiness for my little girl, who had found her prince.

The evening had settled into a quiet calm after the last guest had left, and the embers of the barbecue had long since cooled. The air was heavy with the scent of charred wood and summer night, as I sat in the lounge, sinking into the worn leather of my favourite chair. Everything felt packed away, not

**The Cult's Tentacles**

just the dishes, but the day itself, folded into memories. That's when Judy appeared from her room, her small suitcase clutched in her hand like it carried something far greater than clothes. I looked at her, my voice low. "Are you walking away?" She smiled gently, a little laugh escaping. "No, Dad, we're just going to Trevor's parents'. We'll be back Monday morning." I nodded, my gaze shifting to Trevor who stood awkwardly by the door, hands tucked into his pockets like he wasn't sure if he should be here at all. "Just drive safe," I said, meeting his eyes for a moment longer than necessary. "And make sure you're

**The Cult's Tentacles**

back on Monday before eight." They smiled, wide and carefree, full of the kind of happiness that makes you both proud and wistful at once. I hugged Judy, watching as they got into the car, headlights flickering on, cutting through the dusk as they drove off. And just like that, the yard was empty again, leaving only the hum of cicadas and the faint breeze to fill the space where laughter had been.

Beside me, Karen stood, tears glistening as they slipped down her cheeks. She moved closer, wrapping her arms around me in a tight hug. "Thank you, John," she whispered.

**The Cult's Tentacles**

"They look so happy." I squeezed her back, the weight of her gratitude settling between us. We watched the car's taillights disappear, and then, without a word, turned back toward the house. It was strange, how quickly the life in a home could shift from full to empty. Inside, the silence was thick again. We sat down, the sound of the old couch groaning beneath us. Karen turned to me, her voice soft but steady. "Thank you for giving Trevor the job. He's been so happy. I hope Mr JP will accept him." I grunted, leaning back. "Yeah, we'll see. If he doesn't... well, we'll figure something out."

**The Cult's Tentacles**

A thought began to stir in the back of my mind, nagging at me like an itch. Tomorrow was Sunday. The weight of it suddenly felt heavier than it had in weeks. I stood up abruptly, walking toward the phone, the old rotary dial clicking as I punched in the number. "Who are you calling?" Karen asked her eyes curious but tired.

"The overseer," I muttered, waiting for the familiar voice on the other end. After a few rings, he picked up. "Hello?" "Overseer, it's me. Do I need to go to church tomorrow?" There was a pause. "Yes, why wouldn't you?" "You said you were going to talk to the

**The Cult's Tentacles**

apostle, remember?" My voice was sharper than I intended, laced with the frustration I had tried to suppress all week. "I did. The apostle said I should give you another chance." I hung up with a simple "bye," the doubt lingering in my chest. Had he really spoken to the apostle, or was it all just a way to keep me in line? I turned back toward Karen, who watched me with careful eyes. "He said the apostle told him to give me another chance," I muttered, sinking back into my seat.

Karen smiled faintly. "That's good news." But I couldn't shake the nagging thought. "I wonder if he really

**The Cult's Tentacles**

talked to him," I murmured, more to myself than her. Karen, ever steady, sighed. "It's not our problem, John." I knew she was right, but something inside me wasn't ready to let it go. "There's more to this church, Karen."

She shook her head, walking toward the fridge. "Do you want some ice cream?" I raised an eyebrow, a smirk tugging at the corners of my lips. "Are you trying to cool me down?" "Don't be silly," she said, laughing as she scooped the ice cream into bowls. But in the quiet that followed, the questions lingered—heavy, unanswered, and growing colder by the minute.

**The Cult's Tentacles**

It was a crisp Monday morning when Karen heard the familiar hum of the VW Beetle pulling into the yard. She was in the kitchen, busy with breakfast preparations—the smell of sizzling bacon and fresh coffee filling the air. Wiping her hands on a dish towel, she called out to John. "John! Judy and Trevor are here!" With a flurry of excitement, she rushed to the door, swinging it open just as the young couple stepped out of the car. Smiling, Judy led the way with Trevor trailing behind her. Karen hurried back to the kitchen as Judy and Trevor entered the house, laughter bubbling between them. "Hello, Mom! We're here!" Judy

**The Cult's Tentacles**

called out, her voice bright. Trevor, ever the polite one, added, "It smells amazing in here. I'm starving." Karen beamed as Judy kissed her on the cheek, and Trevor greeted her with a handshake. I stepped into the room, smiling at the sight of them. Judy, her face lighting up, rushed over to hug me. "I love you, Dad," she said, squeezing me tightly. Trevor, looking every bit the professional in his neatly pressed suit, extended his hand. "Good morning, Uncle John." I shook his hand, giving him an approving nod. "You're dressed sharp today," I commented, and he smiled bashfully.

**The Cult's Tentacles**

"Come sit, everyone!" Karen called, ushering us all to the table.

We sat down together, the warmth of family filling the room as we dug into breakfast. Judy talked animatedly about Trevor's family—how thrilled they were that he had landed a job so quickly after graduation. Trevor, though clearly nervous, smiled through it all, nodding along as Judy spoke. "We'll have to see what the boss says," I teased, glancing at Trevor, whose face flushed with nerves.

Judy playfully swatted my arm. "Dad, don't tease him! He's already nervous enough!" After we'd finished eating, I

**The Cult's Tentacles**

turned to Trevor. "Come on, let's head to the office. You can follow me in your car." Trevor nodded, and soon we were pulling into the parking lot. I showed him where to park before leading him straight to my office. As we entered, I pointed him to a chair opposite my desk and sat down, organizing papers and files for the week ahead. Trevor sat quietly, but I could tell he was anxious about the meeting. Once I was ready, I stood up, gesturing for him to follow me down the hallway to my boss's office.

When we arrived, I asked the secretary if we could see him, and after a quick

**The Cult's Tentacles**

phone call, we were waved in. My boss sat behind his large, gleaming desk, the light reflecting off its polished surface. He greeted us with a warm smile.

"How was the graduation, John? And how's Judy doing?" he asked, leaning back in his chair. I smiled. "Both went well, sir. And this here," I gestured to Trevor, "is Judy's fiancé, my future son-in-law." The boss's eyebrows rose with interest. "Ah, I see. Trevor, is it? Did you bring him in to work in the financial sector, John?" Trevor, visibly nervous, nodded.

"Do you have your degree with you?" the boss asked. Trevor quickly pulled

**The Cult's Tentacles**

out his certificate and handed it over. "Yes, sir," he said, his voice steady. The boss scanned it, nodding in approval. "Graduated cum laude, I see. Impressive. Where are you staying, Trevor?" "With my parents in Orkney, sir," Trevor replied. "Orkney!" The boss's face lit up. "Well, that's quite a commute. But Potch is much closer, isn't it?"

He picked up the phone, calling through to his assistant. "Get me Jake at the Potch branch." Turning back to Trevor, the boss said, "I need you over at Potch. You'll report there starting tomorrow." The phone rang, and after

**The Cult's Tentacles**

a quick exchange, the boss confirmed everything with Jake. "He'll be your mentor," he said. "You'll start tomorrow in the office next to the staircase. Don't let me down, Trevor."

"No, sir. Thank you, sir," Trevor said, his voice filled with gratitude. The boss looked at me, signalling that the meeting was over. "John will show you where to go. Good luck." Back in my office, I handed Trevor a piece of paper with the address on it. "Go meet Jake today. He's a good man. You'll do great." Trevor's face broke into a huge smile. "Thank you, Uncle John. I won't disappoint you." As I watched

**The Cult's Tentacles**

him leave, walking towards his car with newfound confidence, I smiled to myself, remembering the first day I had arrived at the company, just as wide-eyed and hopeful as Trevor.

Now that Trevor was settled, heading off to work in Potch, I could finally turn my attention back to my own tasks. There was a sense of relief in knowing that his situation was sorted. With the clock ticking, I still had some time left before the end of the day. I leaned over the keyboard and began typing; pulling up the information I'd been meaning to look into—about the church. It was strange, really. The

**The Cult's Tentacles**

more I delved into it, the more I realized how things had shifted. Once, I'd taken comfort in the familiarity of their teachings. Seeing that they had adopted the Apostolic Creed had reassured me, at first. After all, this creed was nearly universal across traditional Christian denominations, a symbol of unity. But the deeper I looked, the more unsettled I became. After the court case—how had I missed the warning signs?—they had been forced to make changes. Cosmetic changes, some might say, but enough to create a noticeable gap between the original church and this new, splintered version of it—the one I

**The Cult's Tentacles**

was now, to my dismay, entangled with. The most jarring change was the introduction of a new office: the "underdeacon." I stared at the word on the screen, my brow furrowing. The role of deacon was biblical, rooted in scripture. How could they just remove it and replace it with something that had no grounding, no basis in the teachings I knew? Underdeacon. It seemed almost absurd. But yes, this was the work of those apostles who had been excommunicated, who then turned around and restructured everything. It was madness. And then there was the Prophet. That was the hook, wasn't it?

**The Cult's Tentacles**

The lure. They were the only church, they claimed, that had a living prophet. That was the message they used to draw people in, and we—so many of us—had fallen for it. Especially those of us who didn't have a deep understanding of the Bible. We had been caught, drawn in by the promise of something more. A prophet. But what did the Bible really say about prophets? What had Jesus said? I felt a gnawing sense of guilt as I flipped through my Bible, landing on Luke 16:16: "The law and the prophets were until John. "John the Baptist. That was it. The prophets had served their purpose. And then, turning to

**The Cult's Tentacles**

Hebrews 1:1-2, I read again: God no longer sent prophets like in the days of old. I let the words sink in, the truth staring me in the face. The original church, the one I read about, didn't have a prophet. They didn't need one because they understood the Bible. But this splinter group? The one I was now part of? It was a lie. A fake. The realization struck me hard, the words pounding in my mind. I sat there, frozen, waves of shame and regret crashing over me. How had I let it get this far? How had I been so blind? I had neglected my family, spent countless hours devoted to something that was full of secrets and half-truths.

**The Cult's Tentacles**

My heart ached with the weight of it all. Slowly, I locked the computer and gathered my things. The day had been long—too long, really, filled with revelations I hadn't expected. As I pulled the office door shut behind me, the click of the lock seemed to echo louder than usual, closing in on the day, on the lies, on the misplaced trust I had foolishly given.

I walked into the house, the door wide open, a familiar feeling of home washing over me. As soon as I stepped in, Judy was there, phone in hand, waving her fingers in the air. "Hello, Dad!" she shouted, pointing to the

**The Cult's Tentacles**

phone. "It's Trevor!" Her eyes sparkled with excitement. I smiled, nodded, and made my way towards the kitchen. Through the window, I saw Karen in the backyard, taking the washing off the line. When she caught sight of me, her face lit up, and she rushed over to greet me. "I almost forgot the laundry," she said as I walked over to help, reaching for the basket. "This is heavy!" I said with a playful groan as I lifted it. Karen just smiled, shaking her head. "I'm used to it," she replied, tucking a stray hair behind her ear. "That's why you're so strong," I teased, giving her a wink. She laughed, and we carried the basket together into

**The Cult's Tentacles**

the kitchen. I set it down near the counter, but Karen quickly interrupted. "Not here, over there," she pointed towards the ironing board near the back door. "I have to iron it all tomorrow." I grinned, leaning on the counter for a moment. "And I thought you were doing nothing all day." She gave me a mock glare. "All men think that," she replied, but before she could say more, I pulled her close, wrapping my arms around her. "I don't," I whispered. "I love you very much."

Her smile softened, her face glowing with that warmth that always made me feel at home. She kissed me, a soft

**The Cult's Tentacles**

thank you slipping from her lips. Just then, Judy burst in, throwing her arms around me. "Thanks, Dad, for giving Trevor the job! He's so excited. He met his boss today, and everyone was so friendly. He starts tomorrow at 8!" She kissed me on the cheek, her energy contagious.

"That's great, sweetheart," I replied, but before I could say more, Karen interrupted. "John, did you make things right with Kevin today?" I winced. "No, I completely forgot!" I checked the clock—it was 5:30. "Let's go over to the workshop. He closes at 6." I rushed to grab my pen and check book,

**The Cult's Tentacles**

and within minutes, all three of us were driving together to Kevin's workshop. We made it with ten minutes to spare. Kevin was outside, ready to close up shop, but he smiled when he saw us pull up. "Hey there!" he greeted, extending his arm for a handshake that turned into a familiar arm-grab hug. "All three of you, huh?" "Yep," I smiled. "Had to make things right." We followed him into the office, where his wife, Joyce, was busy at her desk. "How much do I owe you?" I asked, getting straight to the point. Kevin shook his head. "You don't owe me anything. Remember the Beetle? I did it for Judy." Judy beamed. "Thank you,

**The Cult's Tentacles**

Uncle Kevin," she said, leaning over to kiss him on the head. His whole face lit up, teeth showing in a big grin. "Thanks, Kev," I added, genuinely grateful. Karen clapped her hands together. "All right, how about we treat you to a Dagwood at the Roadhouse?" Kevin's eyes widened. "The Roadhouse? Wow, I haven't been there in ages. Okay, let's go!"

Joyce, still at her desk, called out, "Wait! I'm still busy!" Kevin waved her off. "That can wait till tomorrow," he said, switching off the lights as we all headed out to the cars. As we piled in, Judy, with a mischievous grin,

**The Cult's Tentacles**

turned to her mom. "So, is that why you didn't make dinner tonight?" Karen chuckled. "Don't tell Dad," she whispered, and we all burst out laughing.

We drove to the Roadhouse, Kevin following us. Once we parked, the windows rolled down, and we chatted back and forth through the open windows like teenagers. I leaned out and said, "Order whatever you want, it's on me." It felt like we were kids again, carefree and enjoying the moment. Joyce, smiling, said, "I forgot how good the food is here." Karen nodded. "Definitely worth the money."

**The Cult's Tentacles**

We ended the evening with milkshakes, laughing and reminiscing, the night drawing to a close in the best way. As we finally parted ways, we waved to Kevin and Joyce, heading home with full hearts and a sense of peace. It was the perfect closure to a long day.

We stepped into the house after a beautiful evening at the roadhouse, the warmth of laughter still lingering in the air. Karen, with her usual gentle smile, offered to make us some coffee. I nodded, feeling the coolness of the night begin to settle into my bones. Judy, quiet as always, sat down next to

**The Cult's Tentacles**

me on the couch, her gaze distant, lost in thought. I shifted, turning toward her. "Now that Trevor is working in Potch,"

I began slowly, "what are you going to do if you get a post in Cape Town?" The words hung heavy between us, and for a moment, she just stared at me, silent and still. I leaned in, my voice softening. "Remember, you're engaged. A relationship separated by thousands of kilometres… it won't survive the storm. It doesn't even work for families." I let the weight of my own words settle. "Look at us. Uncle Alan is down in the Cape, and we've

**The Cult's Tentacles**

lost all contact with him." As if on cue, Karen appeared with the coffee, her brow furrowed. She placed the mugs on the table and spoke with quiet conviction. "I overheard your conversation," she said. "The church played a big role in that." "Mmm," I murmured, a thought tugging at the edges of my mind. "The church..." My voice trailed off as I stood up, walking to the phone. Something deep within me stirred—a decision that had been brewing for a long time, one that could no longer be ignored. I dialled the number, listening to the ringing on the other end. "Hello, good evening, sister. I'd like to speak to the overseer." A

**The Cult's Tentacles**

pause, then, "Okay, thank you. Bye." I hung up, turning to find Karen watching me, curiosity burning in her eyes. "The overseer is with the prophet tonight," I said, my tone flat. "When he comes home, she'll ask him to call me." Karen leaned forward, her voice tentative. "What do you want to talk to him about?" I hesitated for a beat. "I'll tell you later," I said, glancing back at Judy, who was still lost in thought. It seemed like she hadn't considered the gravity of what I was saying.

Finally, she spoke, her voice soft but steady. "But Dad, what should I do?" "You can apply for any teaching post

**The Cult's Tentacles**

in Potchefstroom," I said firmly. "If Trevor doesn't get fired or resign and you're going to get married, he's going to stay there until he retires. People in that company don't leave. They go on pension, or... die before they can."

Karen nodded, her practical side kicking in. "You'd better start applying, Judy. There are only two months left before the new school year starts." Judy's face lit up with sudden determination. She jumped up, kissed me on the forehead, and grinned. "Thank you, Dad. Good night. Night, Mom," she added, planting a kiss on

**The Cult's Tentacles**

Karen's cheek before disappearing down the hallway.

I sipped my coffee, savouring the warmth. "This is the best coffee I've ever had," I said, more to fill the silence than anything else. "Liar," Karen shot back with a teasing smile. "You said that last week too." We chuckled together, the sound soft and familiar in the quiet of the house. But then Karen's face grew serious again. She set her mug down carefully. "What do you want the overseer for?"

I took a deep breath, knowing there was no turning back now. "To resign," I said quietly. Karen's eyes widened,

**The Cult's Tentacles**

shock clear on her face. "What?" Her voice cracked. "But why? After all these years... why now?" I leaned forward, my hands clasped together as if the words I was about to speak were too heavy to release. "This church is a fake, Karen. The true Apostolic don't have a prophet." Her eyes grew even larger, disbelief etched into her features. "You're serious," she whispered. "Yes," I said, my voice steady. "The true church has a deacon. That's the biblical office. But this church removed it, replaced it with some... non-biblical 'underdeacon.'" Karen stared at me, trying to piece it all together. "But... they told us they

**The Cult's Tentacles**

were the only true church," she said, her voice almost breaking. "You mean... they lied to us?" I met her gaze and shook my head slowly. "I don't know anymore." She stood abruptly, the weight of it all too much to bear. "Let's go to bed. He won't call tonight—it's too late." She gathered the empty mugs and headed for the kitchen, her steps heavy with the burden of doubt. As I locked the door behind her, the house felt different. Quieter. Like something had shifted in the air, an old certainty unravelling as the night pressed in around us.

**The Cult's Tentacles**

The morning was still young when I finished shaving, heading to the bedroom. Just as I reached the hallway, the phone rang, sharp and insistent. Judy shot out of her room, darting for the phone like a startled deer, grabbing it just in time. "Hello? Oh, yes. I'll get him. Dad, it's for you." She turned towards me, her voice carrying into the kitchen where Karen was busy with breakfast. I took the receiver from Judy. "Hello, Overseer," I said, keeping my tone even. "I'm fine, thank you. Actually, no, it's not fine. We need to talk." There was a pause. "Alright, tonight then. Goodbye." I hung up and turned to find Karen

**The Cult's Tentacles**

watching me, her face calm but her eyes questioning. "What did he say?" "I'm meeting him tonight, after seven," I replied, the weight of the conversation still hanging over me.

Without a word, Karen turned back to her work. I walked towards the bedroom, feeling the emptiness in my thoughts, moving on autopilot, going through the motions of getting dressed. My mind was a blank slate. By the time I returned to the kitchen, the phone rang again. Judy, quick as lightning, darted past me to grab it once more. "Hello? Oh, I'll call her.

**The Cult's Tentacles**

Mom, it's Aunt Joyce," she said, her shoulders slumping slightly.

I could tell she was waiting for another call, one that mattered more to her. I sat down at the table, mechanically buttering my toast. Karen soon joined me, a smile softening her face as she slipped her arms around me from behind, kissing the top of my head. "What did Joyce want?" I asked my voice light with curiosity. "She wants to know if Judy can help her out in the workshop until she finds a teaching position. I told her I'd ask." Before Karen could turn to Judy, she spoke up. "I don't want to work there,

**The Cult's Tentacles**

Mom," Judy grumbled, her nose wrinkling in distaste. "All they do is rev cars all day." I couldn't help it—I burst into laughter so loud that it became contagious. Karen started giggling, and even Judy cracked a reluctant smile. "Why not?" I teased, turning to Judy. "You could help out. You know cars, right?" Judy shook her head, chuckling. "I don't even have a car, let alone know how to fix one." I leaned back in my chair, a playful grin on my face. "I told you a long time ago. The moment you show me your driver's license, I'll buy you a car." "Oh, Dad," Judy groaned, but there was a hint of amusement in her voice.

**The Cult's Tentacles**

Karen, ever calm, chimed in gently. "Aunt Joyce could use the company, Judy. It's not just about the cars." Judy sighed, glancing towards the phone as it rang again. This time, she stood up slowly and walked over, resignation in her step. She picked it up, her voice softer now. "Hello? How are you?" I stood, giving Karen a quick kiss on the cheek before walking past Judy, who now wore a wide smile, stars twinkling in her eyes as she spoke on the phone. I grinned at her. "Don't keep him late on his first day," I joked. Still smiling, I stepped outside, letting the sunlight wash over me. The brightness felt different today, warmer somehow, as if

**The Cult's Tentacles**

signalling that the days of being trapped under the beast's suffocating grip were numbered. Freedom was near, and with it, a breath of fresh air.

As I drove down the road on my way to the office, the words Alan had spoken a few years ago came rushing back into my mind. "Watch out for that church," he had warned. "It's a cult. They keep people away from their families." His voice had been stern. I hadn't thought much about it back then, but today, the warning lingered, gnawing at the edges of my thoughts. Suddenly, a blaring car horn jolted me back to reality. My heart jumped, and I

**The Cult's Tentacles**

quickly realized the traffic light had turned green. I pressed the gas, shaking off the daze, and sped forward. By the time I reached the office parking lot, I noticed Tom's car parked in its usual spot. I straightened my jacket, still replaying Alan's words in my head, and headed into the office. As I opened the door, there was Tom, waiting for me.

"Hello, Tom," I greeted him. "Hey," he replied with a smile, asking about my family out of routine politeness. "Judy's waiting on a teaching post," I said, feeling the familiar edge of frustration. "Oh," he mused

**The Cult's Tentacles**

thoughtfully, "you know, the headmaster of one of the small schools out near the smallholdings is one of my clients. I can ask him about any openings." "That would be great, thank you." My spirits lifted a little at the possibility.

After some small talk, Tom's expression turned serious. "The boss wants me to run the Fochville branch," he said. "My position as district auditor will be open soon. You interested?" I shook my head, the answer already formed in my mind. "No thanks. I'm happy where I am." "Why not?" He looked at me, eyebrows raised, sensing

**The Cult's Tentacles**

there was more to my refusal. "I don't want to be sleeping out of town all the time," I said, not really telling him the whole truth. Tom narrowed his eyes, reading between the lines. "Is it the church?" he asked. "Do they need to give you permission for something like that?" His words hit me harder than I expected. He wasn't entirely wrong. "You're right about the permission thing," I admitted. "But no, it's not because of that. I'm actually resigning from the church. Tonight." Tom blinked, surprised. "Oh? What made you decide that?"

**The Cult's Tentacles**

I sighed, my mind flashing through the endless nights of doubt, the moments I had started to see through the teachings that once seemed so solid. "I did some digging into their history and realized… they're built on lies." Tom let out a soft whistle, clapping his hands. "Wow. And it took you nearly thirty years to see it?" I chuckled bitterly. "You know, when you're part of something for so long, you don't notice the cracks. But once you step outside and really look in…" I trailed off, shaking my head. He nodded, understanding. "Well, better late than never, right?" We wrapped up our conversation, and as Tom got up to

**The Cult's Tentacles**

leave, he promised to speak to his client about Judy's teaching post. After he left, I leaned back in my chair, his job offer still hanging in the air. It wasn't for me. Once I settled back into work, my thoughts drifted again, this time to the research I'd been doing on the church's practices. I opened my computer, typing in keywords, digging deeper. Sealing services, baptisms for the dead, giving the Holy Spirit to people who had passed on—it all sounded strange, even sacrilegious. I found myself in disbelief at how long I had accepted these practices without questioning them. Then I stumbled on a verse that shook me to the core. Acts

**The Cult's Tentacles**

2:17—"And it shall come to pass in the last days, saith God, I will pour out of my Spirit upon all flesh." Not spirits. Not the dead. Flesh. Living, breathing people. What had I been a part of? Baptizing a living person for a dead one? Giving the Holy Ghost to those who had already passed on? It felt wrong, twisted even. "What could a dead person do with the Holy Spirit?"I thought, my hands clenching the edges of the desk. The Bible itself said the dead knew nothing. I leaned back in my chair, letting out a deep breath. This was it. Tonight, I would walk away for good. As the day wound down, I closed my computer and

**The Cult's Tentacles**

locked the office door. Walking down the passage, I felt a strange surge of relief, like a weight had been lifted off my chest. My fists clenched in excitement, and before I knew it, I was punching the air, shouting "Yes!" as I strode down the hallway Tonight's meeting with the overseer would be the final chapter in this story. And after that, I would be free.

The late afternoon sun filtered through the windshield, casting a golden hue over the world as I drove home. There was something different about the light today, something softer, clearer. The birds swooped through the air with

**The Cult's Tentacles**

effortless grace, and the sun, dipping slowly toward the horizon, painted the sky in fiery streaks of orange and pink. People walking along the roadside seemed more animated, more alive, like they were part of some grander picture I had missed before. As I turned into our yard, even the house looked beautiful, bathed in the fading sunlight. Its familiar structure felt like a warm embrace, comforting in its simplicity. I parked the car and stepped out, breathing in the crisp evening air. Judy, my daughter, came out to greet me, her smile wide and welcoming. She no longer wore the ponytail she had when she was younger, though it

**The Cult's Tentacles**

felt like only yesterday. "Hello, Dad," she said, her voice filled with joy. I hugged her, feeling the warmth of her embrace, and as I did, the aroma from the kitchen wafted toward me. It was marvellous—rich and savoury, a promise of a meal prepared with care. Karen, my wife, appeared in the doorway, a quick kiss on my cheek as she said, "Dinner's ready. You've got an appointment soon; let's eat so you won't be late."

I turned and watched as the last rays of the sun slipped behind the horizon, the sky now a brilliant blend of purples and blues. It was a beautiful, fleeting

**The Cult's Tentacles**

moment, and I let it settle in my mind before going inside to join my family. Sitting at the table, I couldn't help but exclaim, "Mmm, this is a meal fit for a king. "Karen laughed softly as she sat down. "It's a meal for a free man," she said with a knowing smile.

I chuckled, and we began to eat. She asked me about my day, and after a moment, I told her, "I turned down a promotion again. "Karen didn't seem surprised. "Tom's job?" she asked. I nodded. "Yeah, they offered it to me, but I don't want it. His job means sleeping away from home, and I'm not interested in that. "Karen smiled, her

**The Cult's Tentacles**

eyes full of understanding. "Joyce stopped by this morning. She asked Judy to help her out with something."

I looked at Judy. "Did you enjoy it? "She shrugged, but there was a twinkle in her eye. "It wasn't bad, but I prefer being in a classroom." "Mmm, maybe a classroom in a small farm school?" I suggested. Her face lit up at the thought. "That would be nice," she said, her smile wide. Family. It was precious—something I held close, especially in moments like these. But time was slipping away, and I knew I had somewhere to be. I glanced at the clock. "It's nearly seven. I need to take

**The Cult's Tentacles**

care of something." I stood and kissed them both before heading out the door. "I'll be back soon." As I drove down the road, the streetlights flickered on, casting soft yellow circles on the pavement. Everything felt different, calm even, though I was on my way to confront something that had always filled me with tension. The overseer. And, as it seemed, the evangelist too—his car was already parked in the driveway when I arrived. I stepped out of the car, closing the door softly, not wanting to disturb the quiet that hung in the air. The sister opened the door, her face a mask of polite curiosity, and led me inside. They were both seated

**The Cult's Tentacles**

in their usual spots, the overseer and the evangelist, waiting. We exchanged pleasantries, but the air was thick with anticipation. They knew why I was there. Finally, I broke the silence. "I'm here to tell you that I'm resigning from the church. "The room froze. It felt as if time itself had stopped. The evangelist blinked in disbelief. "Come again?" "I'm resigning," I repeated, my voice steady, calm. The overseer cleared his throat, his voice much softer than usual. "Do you know what you're saying?" He didn't wait for me to answer. "You're turning your back on your salvation. This church is Christ, and if you leave, you'll be

**The Cult's Tentacles**

damned." The evangelist leaned forward, his face stern. "You'll lose all your blessings. Do you realize that?" I stood my ground, unshaken. "The church that is the body of Christ is not this church. This church is built on lies. And before I go, I just want to say that staying here will cost you your salvation." I paused, letting my words sink in. "I don't need anyone's permission to leave."

I turned to go, but before I reached the door, the evangelist called out, "You'll always be apostolic, no matter what." I smiled, not even looking back. "Maybe you will. But I'm free." As I drove

**The Cult's Tentacles**

home, a sense of peace settled over me, deeper than anything I'd felt before. The weight I'd been carrying for so long had lifted. When I pulled into the driveway, I could see Karen and Judy waiting for me inside. The moment I walked through the door, I couldn't contain myself. "We're free!" I shouted, a grin spreading across my face. Karen jumped up, laughing, while Judy shouted, "Yippee!" The air was electric with joy, and for the first time in years, I felt completely unburdened. "We need ice cream to celebrate," Karen declared, heading to the kitchen. Judy grinned and asked, "Dad, can I go to Trevor's parents' service this

**The Cult's Tentacles**

weekend?" "Are they apostolic?" I asked, teasingly. "No, they're baptized." I nodded. "No problem, then. "Thanks, Dad." Judy rushed off to help her mom in the kitchen. As I watched them, I couldn't help but feel an overwhelming sense of gratitude. We had escaped the" Tentacles" that had bound us for so long, and now, as we sat around the table, bowls of ice cream in hand, We laughed and celebrated our newfound freedom— together.

"*God the Father, God the Son, and God the Holy Spirit deserve all the praise and honour for making this book possible.*"